Philip Doddridge

Sermons on the Religious Education of Children

Preached at Northampton

Philip Doddridge

Sermons on the Religious Education of Children
Preached at Northampton

ISBN/EAN: 9783337084271

Printed in Europe, USA, Canada, Australia, Japan

Cover: Foto ©Lupo / pixelio.de

More available books at **www.hansebooks.com**

SERMONS

ON THE

RELIGIOUS EDUCATION

OF

CHILDREN,

PREACHED AT NORTHAMPTON.

BY PHILIP DODDRIDGE, D. D.

AMHERST, NEWHAMPSHIRE,
PRINTED AND SOLD BY SAMUEL CUSHING.
M,DCC,XCVII.

EXTRACTS from D. SOME's recommendatory Preface to the following Sermons.—

'THE neglect of the rising generation, which so generally prevails, ought, surely, to awaken our serious concern for it; and I persuade myself that the present attempt will be welcome to all who are duly impressed with that concern; for so far as I am capable of judging, it is well adapted to answer its intended purposes.

"As the subject of these sermons is no matter of controversy, but plain and important duty, one would hope they will not fall under the severe censure of any. At least I am persuaded that humble and serious christians, whose chief concern is to know and do their duty, will find agreeable entertainment, and much profitable instruction in the perusal of them.

SERMON I.

ON THE EDUCATION OF CHILDREN.

PROV. XXII. 6.

Train up a Child in the way he should go: and when he is old he will not depart from it.

IT is a most amiable and instructive part of the character which Isaiah draws of *the great shepherd* of the church, that *he should gather the Lambs with his arm, and carry them in his bosom;* A representation abundantly answered by the tender care which our Redeemer expressed for the weakest of his disciples; and beautifully illustrated by the endearing condescension, with which he embraced and blessed little infants. Nor is it foreign to the present purpose to observe, that when he recommends to Peter the care of his flock, as the most important and acceptable evidence of his sincere affection to his person, he varies the phrase: in one place saying, *feed my sheep,* and in the other, *feed my lambs.*—Perhaps it might be intended in part to intimate, that the care of a gospel minister, who would, in the most agreeable manner, approve his love to his master, should extend itself to the rising generation, as well as to those of a maturer age, and more considerable standing in the church. It is in obedience to his authority, and from a regard to his interest, that I am now entering on the work of catechising, which I shall introduce with some practical discourses, *on the education of children,* the subject which is now before us.

I persuade myself, that you, my friends, will not be displeased to hear that I intend to handle it at large, and to make it the employment of more than a single Sabbath. A little reflection may convince you, that I could hardly offer any thing to your consideration of greater importance; and that humanly speaking, there is nothing in which the comfort of families, the prosperity of nations, the salvation of souls, the interest of a Redeemer, and the glory of God, is more apparently and intimately concerned.

I very readily allow, that no human endeavors, either of ministers or parents, can ever be effectual, to bring one soul to the saving knowledge of God in Christ, without the co-operating and transforming influences of the blessed spirit: yet you well know, and I hope you seriously consider, that this does not in the least weaken our obligation to the most diligent use of proper means. The great God has stated rules of operation in the world of grace, as well as of nature; and though he is not limited to them, it is arrogant, and may be destructive, to expect that he should deviate from them in favor of us or ours.

We live not by bread alone, but by every word that proceedeth out of the mouth of God: and were he determined to continue your lives, or the lives of your children, he could, no doubt, feed or support you by miracle: Yet you think yourselves obliged to a prudent care for your daily bread, and justly conclude that were you to neglect to administer it to your infant offspring, you would be chargeable with their murder before God and man; nor could you think of pleading it as any excuse that you referred them to a miraculous Divine care, whilst you left them destiute of any human supplies. Such a plea would only add impiety to cruelty, and greatly aggravate the crime it attempted to palliate. As absurd would it be for us to flatter ourselves with a hope that our children should be taught of God, and regenerated and sanctified by the influences of his grace, if we neglect that prudent and religious care in their education, which it is my business this day to describe and recommend, and which Solomon urges in the words of my text: *Train up a child in the way in which he should go; and when he is old he will not depart from it.*

I need not offer you many critical remarks on so plain and intelligible a passage. You will easily observe, that it consists of an important advice, addressed to the parents and governors of Children. *Train up a child in the way which he should go;* and also of a weighty reason by which it is enforced, *and when he is old he will not depart from it.*

The general sense is undoubtedly retained in our translation, as it commonly is;

but here, as in many other places, something of the original energy and beauty is lost.

The Hebrew word, which we render *train up*, does sometimes signify in the general, to initiate into some science or discipline; and very frequently to apply any new thing to the use for which it was intended. It is especially used of sacred things which were solemnly dedicated or set apart to the service of God: And perhaps it may here be intended to intimate that a due care is to be taken in the education of our children, from a principle of religion, as well as of prudence and humanity; and that our instructions should lead them to the knowledge of God, and be adapted to form them for his service, as well as to engage them to personal and social virtue.

It is added, that a child should be trained up *in the way in which he should go;* which seems to be more exactly rendered by others, at the entrance, or from the beginning of his way, to express the early care which ought to be taken to prevent the prevalency of irregular habits, by endeavoring from the first dawning of reason to direct it aright, and to infuse into the tender unpractised mind, the important maxims of wisdom and goodness.

To encourage us to this care, the Wise Man assures us that we may reasonably expect the most happy consequence from it: That if the young traveller be thus directed to set out well in the journey of life, there is a fair prospect that he will go on to its most distant stages with increasing honor and happiness.—*Train up a child in the way he should go; and when he is old, he will not depart from it.*

I shall endeavor to illustrate and enforce this important advice in the following method, which appears to me the most natural, and for that reason the most eligible.

I. I shall more particularly mark out the way in which children are to be trained up.

II. Offer some plain and serious considerations to awaken you to this pious and necessary care.

III. Direct to the manner in which the attempt is to be made, and the precautions which are to be used in order to render it effectual.

And then;

IV. I will conclude the whole with a more particular application suited to your different characters, relations, and circumstances of life.

I am very sensible that it is a very delicate as well as important subject, which is now before me; I have therefore thought myself obliged more attentively to weigh what has occurred to my own meditations more diligently to consult the sentiments of others, and above all more earnestly to seek those divine influences, without which I know I am unequal to the easiest task; but in dependance on which, I cheerfully attempt one of the most difficult. The result of the whole I humbly offer to your candid examination; not pretending at any time to dictate in an authoritative manner, and leaſt of all on ſuch an occaſion as this; but rather ſpeaking as to wiſe men, who are themſelves to judge what I ſay. May the divine aſſiſtance and bleſſing attend us in all!

Firſt, I am to deſcribe the way in which children are to be trained up.

Our tranſlation, as I have told you, though not very literal, is agreeable to the ſenſe of the original, *The way in which the child ſhould go*. And undoubtedly this is no other than the good old way; the way of ſerious practical religion; the way which God has in his word marked out for us; the way which all the children of God have trodden in every ſucceeding age; the way, the only way in which we and ours can find reſt to our ſouls.

But it is not proper to leave the matter thus generally explained. I would therefore more particularly obſerve:—that it is the way of piety to God—and of faith in our Lord Jeſus Chriſt;—the way of obedience to parents—and of benevolence to all, the way of dilligence—and of integrity;—the way of humility—and of ſelf-denial. I am perſuaded that each of theſe particulars will deſerve your ſerious attention and regard.

1. Children ſhould undoubtedly be trained up in the way of piety and devotion towards God.

This, as you well know, is the ſum and the foundation of every thing truly good. *The fear of the Lord is the beginning of wiſdom*. The Pſalmiſt therefore invites the children to him, with the promise of instructing them in it; *Come ye Children, hearken unto me, and I will teach you the fear of the Lord.* And it is certain some right notions of the Supreme Being must be implanted in the minds of children, before there can be a reasonable foundation for teaching them those doctrines which peculiarly relate to Christ under the character of the mediator; for he that comes unto God (by him) must believe that he is, and that he is the rewarder of them that diligently seek him.

The proof of the Being of God, and some of those attributes of the divine nature in which we are most concerned, depends on such easy principles, that I cannot but think the weakest might enter into it. A child will easily apprehend that as every house is built by some man, and there can be no work without an author; so *he that built all things is God.* And from this obvious idea of God as the maker of all, we may naturally represent him as very great and very good, that they may be taught at once to reverence and love him.

It is of great importance, that children early imbibe an awe of God, and an humble veneration for his perfections and glories. He ought therefore to be represented to them as the great *Lord of all*; and when we take occasion to mention to them other invisible agents, whether Angels or Devils, we should, as Dr. Watts has most judiciously observed, always represent them as entirely under the government and controul of God, that no sentiments of admiration of good spirits, or terror of the bad, may distract their tender minds, or infringe on those regards which are the incommunicable prerogative of the *Great Supreme*.

There should be a peculiar caution, that when we teach these infant tongues to pronounce that great and terrible name, *the Lord our God*, they may not learn to take it in vain; but may use it with a becoming solemnity, as remembering that we and they are *but dust and ashes before him*.—When I hear the little creatures speaking of " the great God, the blessed God, the glorious God," as I sometimes do, it gives me a sensible pleasure, and I consider it as a probable proof of great wisdom and piety in those who have the charge of their education.

Yet great care should be taken not to confine our discourses to these awful views, lest the dread of God should so fall upon them, as that his excellencies should make them afraid to approach him. We should describe him as not only the greatest, but the best of beings. We should teach them to know him by the most encouraging name of *the Lord, the Lord God, merciful and gracious, long-suffering, and abundant in goodness and truth, keeping mercy for thousands, and forgiving iniquity, transgression and sin*. We should represent him as the universal, kind, indulgent parent, who loves his creatures, and by all proper methods provides for their happiness. And we should particularly represent his goodness to them, with what more than parental tenderness he watched round their cradles; with what compassion he heard their feeble cries, before their infant thoughts could form themselves into prayer: We should tell them that they live every moment on God; and that all our affection for them is no more than he puts into our hearts; and all our power to help them is no more than he lodges in our hands.

We should also solemnly remind them that in a very little while their spirits are to return to this God; that as he is now always with them and knows every thing they do, or speak, or think, so he will bring every work into judgment, and make them forever happy or miserable, as they on the whole are found obedient or rebellious. And here the most lively and pathetic descriptions, which the scriptures give us of Heaven and of Hell, should be laid before them, and urged on their consideration.

When such a foundation is laid in the belief of the providence of God, and of a future state both of rewards and punishments, children should be instructed in the duty they owe to God, and should be particularly taught to pray to him, and to praise him. It would be best of all, if, from a deep sense of his perfections, and their own necessities, they could be engaged to breathe out their souls before him in words of their own, were they ever so weak and broken. Yet you will readily allow, that till this can be expected, it may be very proper to teach them some form of prayer and thankfgiving, confifting of such plain scriptures, or other familiar expreffions, as may beft fuit their circumftances and underftandings. If the Lord's Prayer be taught them, as a form, I hope you will confider how comprehenfive the expreffions are; how faft the ideas rife and vary; and confequently how neceffary it is, that it be frequently, and largely explained to them; left the repetition of it degenerate into a mere ceremony, as I fear it does amongft many, who are perhaps moft zealous for its ufe.

But what I have faid on this head of piety and devotion, muft be confidered in an infeparable conneƈtion with what I am to add under the next.

2. Children muft be trained up in the way of faith in the Lord Jefus Chrift.

You know, my friends, and I hope many of you know it to the daily joy of your fouls, that Chrift is the way, the truth, and the life; and that it is by him we have boldnefs and accefs with confidence to a God who might otherwife appear as a confuming fire. It is therefore of great importance to lead children betimes into the knowledge of Chrift, which is, no doubt, a confiderable part of that nurture and admonition of the Lord, which the Apoftle recommends, and was perhaps what he principally intended by the words.

We should therefore teach them betimes that the first parents of the human race, most ungratefully rebelled against God, and subjected themselves and all their offspring to his wrath and curse. The awful consequences of this should be opened at large, and we should labor to convince them that they have made themselves liable to the divine displeasure (that dreadful thing!) by their own personal guilt; and thus by the knowledge of the law should we make way for the gospel, the joyful news of the deliverance by Christ.

In unfolding this, great care ought to be taken that we do not fill their minds with an aversion to one Sacred Person, while we endeavour to attract their regards to another. The Father is not to be represented as severe, and almost inexorable; hardly prevailed upon by the intercession of his compassionate Son, to entertain thoughts of mercy and forgiveness. Far from that, we should speak of him as the overflowing fountain of goodness, whose eye pitied us in our helpless distress, whose almighty arm was stretched out for our rescue, whose eternal counsels of wisdom and love formed that important scheme, to which we owe all our hopes. I have often had occasion to shew you at large that this is the scripture doctrine; our children should be early taught it, and taught what that scheme was, so far as their understandings can receive it, and ours can explain it, we should often repeat it to them, that God is so holy, and yet so gracious.

B.

rather than he would on the one hand deſtroy man, or on the other leave ſin unpuniſhed, he made his own Son a ſacrifice for it, appointing him to be humbled, that we might be exalted, to die that we might live.

We ſhould alſo repreſent to them, (with holy wonder and joy) how readily the Lord Jeſus Chriſt conſented to procure our deliverance in ſo expenſive a way. How chearfully he ſaid, *Lo, I come; I delight to do thy will, O my God!* To enhance the value of this amazing love, we ſhould endeavour according to our weak capacities, to teach them who this compaſſionate Redeemer is; to repreſent ſomething of his glories as the eternal Son of God, and the great Lord of angels and men. We ſhould inſtruct them in his amazing condeſcenſion in laying aſide theſe glories, that he might become a little, weak, helpleſs child, and afterwards an afflicted ſorrowful man. We ſhould lead them into the knowledge of thoſe circumſtances of the hiſtory of Jeſus, which may have the greateſt tendency to ſtrike their minds, and to impreſs them with an early ſenſe of gratitude and love to him. We ſhould tell them how poor he made himſelf, that he might enrich us; how diligently he went about doing good, how willingly he preached the goſpel to the loweſt of the people. And we ſhould eſpecially tell them how kind he was to little children, and how he chid his diſciples when they would have hindered them from being brought to him: It is expreſsly said, *Jesus was much displeased, and said, suffer little children to come unto me, and forbid them not, for of such is the kingdom of God.* A tender circumstance, for which perhaps was recorded (in part at least) for this very reason that children in succeeding ages might be impressed and affected with it.

Through these scenes of his life we should lead them on to his death: We should shew how easily he could have delivered himself (of which he gave so sensible an evidence) in striking down by one word, those who came to apprehend him; and yet how patiently he submitted to the most cruel injuries to be scourged and spit upon, to be crowned with thorns, and to bear the cross. We should shew them how this innocent, holy, divine person was *brought as a lamb to the slaughter*; and while they were piercing him with nails, instead of loading them with curses, he prayed for them, saying, *Father forgive them, for they know not what they do*. And when their little hearts are awed and melted, with so strange a story, we should tell them, it was thus he groaned and bled, and died for us, and often remind them of their own concern in what was then transacted.

We should lead on their thoughts to the glorious views of Christ's resurrection and ascension; and tell them with what adorable goodness he still remembers his people in the midst of his exaltation; pleading the cause of sinful creatures, and employing his interest in the court of Heaven, to procure life and glory for all that believe in him and love him.

We should then go on to instruct them in those particulars of obedience, by which the sincerity of our faith and our love is to be approved; at the same time reminding them of their own weakness, and telling them how God helps us, by sending his holy spirit to dwell in our hearts, to furnish us for every good word and work. An important lesson, without attending to which our instruction will be vain, and their hearing will likewise be vain!

3. Children should be trained up in the way of obedience to their parents.

This is a command which God recommended from Mount Sinai by annexing to it a particular promise of long life; a blessing which young persons greatly desire. The Apostle therefore observes, that it is *the first commandment with promise*; i. e. a command eminently remarkable for the manner in which the promise is adjoined. And it is certainly a wise constitution of Providence that gives so much to parental authority, especially while children are in their younger years, their minds being then incapable of judging and acting for themselves in matters of importance. Children should therefore be early taught and convinced by scripture, that God has committed them into the hands of their parents; and consequently, that reverence and obedience to their parents, is a part of the duty they owe to God, and disobedience to them is rebellion against him. And parents should by no means indulge their children in a direct and resolute opposition to their will in matters of greater or smaller moment; remembering that a child left to himself brings his parents to shame, and himself to ruin; and with regard to subjection, as well as affection, *it is good for a man to bear the yoke in his youth.*

4. Children should be trained up in the way of benevolence and kindness to all.

The great Apostle tells us that *love is the fulfilling of the law,* and that all those branches of it which relate to our neighbor, are comprehended in that one word love. This love therefore we should endeavor to teach them; and we shall find that in many instances, it will be a law to itself; and guide them right in many particular actions, the obligations to which may depend on principles of equity, which lie far beyond the reach of their feeble understandings. There is hardly an instruction relating to our duty more happily adapted to the capacity of children, than that golden law (so important to all of the maturest age) *Whatsoever ye would that others should do unto you, do ye so unto them.* This rule we should teach them, and by this should examine their actions. From their cradles we should often inculcate it upon them, that a great deal of religion consists in doing good; that *the wisdom from above is full of mercy and good fruits;* and that every christian should do good unto all as he has opportunity.

That such instructions may be welcome to them, we should endeavor, by all prudent methods, to soften their hearts to sentiments of humanity and tenderness; and guard against every thing that would have a contrary tendency. We should remove from them as much as possible all kind of cruel and bloody spectacles, and should carefully discourage any thing barbarous in their treatment of brute creatures; by no means allowing them to sport themselves in the death or pain of domestic animals, but rather teaching them to treat the poor creatures kindly, and take care of them; the contrary to which is a detestable sign of a savage and malignant disposition, the merciful man regardeth the life of his beast.

We should likewise take care to teach them the odiousness and folly of a selfish temper, and encourage them in a willingness to impart to others what is agreeable and entertaining to themselves: Especially we should endeavor to form them to sentiments of compassion for the poor. We should shew them where God has said, *Blessed is the man that considereth the poor, the Lord will remember him in the day of trouble. He that hath pity upon the poor lendeth to the Lord, and that which he hath given will he pay him again.* And we should shew them by our own practices, that we verily believe these promises to be true and important. It might not be improper sometimes to make our children the messengers by which we send some small supply to the indigent and distressed; and if they discover a disposition to give something out of the little stock we allow them to call their own, we should joyfully encourage it, and should take care that they never lose by their charity, but that in a prudent manner we abundantly repay it. It is hardly to be imagined that children thus brought up, should, in the advance of life, prove injurious and oppressive; they will rather be the ornaments of religion, and blessings to the world, and probably will be in the number of the last whom Providence will suffer to want.

5. *Children should be trained up in the way of diligence.*

This should undoubtedly be our care, if we have any regard to the welfare either of their bodies or their souls. In whatever station of life they may at length be fixed, it is certain there is little prospect of their acquitting themselves with usefulness, honor and advantage without a close and resolute application; whereas, the wisest of princes and of men has said, *Seest thou a man diligent in his business? he shall stand before kings, he shall not stand before mean men,* and it is evident that a diligent prosecution of business keeps one out of the way of a thousand temptations, which idleness seems to invite, leading a man into numberless instances of vice and folly because he has nothing else to do.

A prudent and religious parent will therefore be concerned that his children may not early contract so pernicious a habit, nor enter upon life like persons that have no business in it but to crowd the stage, and stand in the way of those who are better employed.—Instead of suffering them to saunter about from place to place (as abundance of young people do, to no imaginable purpose of usefulness, or even of entertainment) he would quickly assign them some employment for their time: An employment so moderated, and so diversified, as not to overwhelm and fatigue their tender spirits; yet sufficient to keep them wakeful and active. Nor is this so difficult as some may imagine; for children are a busy kind of creatures, naturally fond of learning new things, and trying and shewing what they can do. So that I am persuaded, were perfect inactivity to be imposed upon them as a penance but for one hour, they would be heartily weary of it, and would be glad to seek their refuge from it, in almost any business you would think fit to employ them about.

Thus should they be disciplined in their infant years, should early be taught the value of time, and early accustomed to improve it, till they grow fit for some calling in life; in which they should at length be placed with this important maxim deeply engraven upon their minds, "That full employ in whatever service they are fixed, is a thing by no means to be dreaded, but on the contrary, greatly to be desired."

I shall conclude this head with the mention of a very remarkable law amongst the

Athenians, which ordained "That those, who had been brought up to no employ by their parents, should not be obliged to keep them, if they came to want in their old age; which all other (legitimate) children were."

6. Children should be trained up in the way of integrity.

Simplicity and godly sincerity is not only a very amiable, but an essential part of the christian character; and we are every one of us indispensably obliged to prove ourselves *Israelites indeed, in whom there is no allowed guile.* And this is a circumstance that will peculiarly require our regard in the education of our children, and of all young persons under our care.

It is very melancholy to observe, how soon the artifices and deceits of corrupt nature begin to discover themselves. In this respect we are transgressors from the womb, and go astray almost as soon as we are born, speaking lies. Great care therefore should be taken to form the minds of children to a love for truth and candour, and a sense of the meanness as well as the guilt of a lie. We should be cautious, that we do not expose them to any temptations of this kind, either by unreasonable severities, on account of little faults, or by hasty surprizes, when enquiring into any matter of fact, which it may seem their interests to disguise by a falsehood; And when we find them guilty of a known and deliberate lie, we should express our horror of it, not only by a present reproof or correction; but by such a conduct towards them for some time afterwards, as may plainly show them how greatly we are amazed, grieved and displeased. When so solemn a business is made of the first faults of this kind, it may be a mean of preventing many more.

I will further add, that we ought not only thus severely animadvert upon a direct lie but likewise, in a proper degree, to discourage all kinds of equivocations and double meanings, and those little tricks and artifices by which they may endeavour to impose on each other, or on those that are older than themselves. We should often inculcate upon them that excellent scripture, *He that walketh uprightly, walketh surely; but he that perverteth his way,* (that twists and distorts it with the perplexities of artifice and deceit) *shall at length be known.* Be showing them every day, how easy, how pleasant, how honorable, and how advantageous it is to maintain a fair, open, honest temper; and on the other hand, what folly there is in cunning and dishonesty in all its forms; and how certain it is, that by studying and practising it, they take the readiest way to make themselves anxious and useless, infamous and odious. Above all, should we remind them, that the righteous Lord loveth righteousness, and his favourable countenance beholdeth the upright; but lying lips are such an abomination to him, that he expressly declares, *all liars shall have their part in the lake which burns with fire and brimstone.*

7. Children should be trained up in the way of humility.

This is a grace, which our Lord particularly invites us to learn of him, and most frequently recommends to us; well knowing that without it, so humbling a scheme as he came to introduce, would never meet with a welcome reception. And with regard to the present life, it is a most lovely ornament, which engages universal esteem and affection; so that before honour is humility: On the whole we find, *He that exalteth himself is abased, and he that humbleth himself is exalted*, both by God and man.

A regard therefore to the ease, honour, and happiness of our children, should engage us to an early endeavour of checking that pride, which was the first sin, and the ruin of our natures; and diffuses itself so wide, and sinks so deep, into all that draw their original from degenerate Adam. We should teach them to express humility and modesty in their converse with all.

They should be taught to treat their superiors with peculiar respect, and should at proper seasons be accustomed to silence and reserve before them. Hence they will learn in some degree the government of the tongue, a branch of wisdom, which in the advance of life will be of great importance to the quiet of others, and to their own comfort and reputation.

Nor should they be allowed to assume airs of insolence towards their equals; but rather be taught to yield, to oblige, and to give up their right for the sake of peace. To this purpose I cannot but think it desirable, that they should be generally accustomed to treat each other with those forms of civility and complaisance which are usual among well bred people in their rank of life. I know these things are mere trifles in themselves, yet they are the outguards of humanity and friendship, and effectually prevent many a rude attack, which, taking its rise from some little circumstances, may nevertheless be attended with fatal consequences. I thought it proper to mention this here, because (as *Scougal* very justly and elegantly expresses it) "These modes are the shadows of humility, and seem intended to shew our regard for others, and the low thoughts we have of ourselves."

I shall only add further, that it is great imprudence and unkindness to children, to indulge them in a haughty and imperious behavior towards those who are most their inferiors. They should be made to understand, that the servants of the family are not their servants, nor to be under their government and controul. I then rather insist upon this, because I have generally observed that where young people have been permitted to tyrannize over persons in the lowest circumstances of life, the humour has shamefully grown upon them, till it has diffused insolence and arrogance through their behavior to all about them.

Lastly, children should be trained up in the way of self denial.

As without something of this temper we can never follow Christ, or expect to be owned by him as his disciples; so neither indeed can we pass comfortably through the world. For whatever unexperienced youth may dream, a great many distasteful and mortifying circumstances will occur in life, which will unhinge our minds almost every hour, if we cannot manage, and in many instances deny our appetites, our passions, and our humours. We should therefore endeavor to teach our children this important lesson betimes; and if we succeed in our care, we shall leave them abundantly richer and happier, in this rule and possession of their own spirits, than the most plentiful estates, or the most unlimited power over others could make them.

When a rational creature becomes the slave of appetite, he sinks beneath the dignity of the human nature, as well as the sanctity of the christian profession. It is therefore observable, that when the apostle mentions the three grand branches of practical religion, he puts sobriety in the front; perhaps to intimate, that where that is neglected, the other cannot be suitably regarded. "*The Grace of God* (i. e. the Gospel) *teaches us to live soberly, righteously and godly.*" Children therefore, as well as young men, should be exhorted to be sober minded: And they should be taught it by early self denial. It is certain that if their own appetite and taste were to determine the kind and quantity of their food, many of them would quickly destroy their constitution, and perhaps their lives; since they have often the greatest desire for those things which are the most improper. And it seems justly observed by a very wise man (who was himself a melancholy instance of it). "That the fondness of mothers for their children in letting them eat and drink what they will, lays a foundation for most of those calamities in human life which proceed from bodily indisposition." Nay, I will add, that it is the part of wisdom and love, not only to deny what would be unwholesome, but to guard against indulging them in too great a nicety either of food or dress, people of sense cannot but see if they would please to consider it, that to know how to fare plainly, and sometimes a little hardly, carries a man with ease and pleasure through many circumstances of life, which to luxury and delicacy would be almost intolerable.

The government of the passions is another branch of self-denial, to which children should early be habituated, and so much the rather, because in an age when reason is so weak, the passions are apt to appear with peculiar force and violence. A prudent care should therefore be taken to repress the exorbitancies of them. For which purpose it is of great importance, that they never be suffered to carry any point, by obstinacy noise and clamour, which is indeed to bestow a reward on a fault that deserves a severe reprimand. Nay, I will venture to add, that though it be very inhuman to take pleasure in making them uneasy by needless mortifications, yet they are eagerly and intemperately desirous of a trifle, they ought, for that very reason sometimes to be denied it, to teach them more moderation for the future. And if by such methods they gradually learn to conquer their little humours and fancies, they learn no inconsiderable branch of true fortitude and wisdom. I cannot express this better than in the words of Mr. Locke, in his excellent treatise on the subject before us; " He that has found out the way to keep a child's spirit easy, active and free, and yet at the same time to restrain him from many things which he has a mind to, and draw him to things uneasy to him, has got the true secret of education."

I have sometimes been surprised to see how a fair sense of honor and praise has carried some children of a generous temper in a long and resolute course of self-denial. But undoubtedly the noblest principle of all is a sense of religion. Happy would it indeed be if they were led to see, that there is but very little in this kind of gratifications and indulgences that the world itself is but a poor empty trifle; and that the great thing a rational creature should be concerned about, is to please God, and get well to Heaven. May divine grace teach us this important lesson for ourselves, that we may transmit it with the greatest advantage to our children! AMEN.

SERMON II.

ON THE EDUCATION OF CHILDREN.

PROV. XXII. 6.

Train up a Child in the way he should go; and when he is old he will not depart from it.

IT is certainly a very pleasing reflection to every faithful minister of the gospel, that the cause, in which he is engaged, is the most benevolent, as well as the most religious; subserving the glory of God by promoting happiness of mankind. It must be a great satisfaction to a man of integrity and humanity to think that it is not his business to dazzle and confound his hearers with the artifices of speech, to give the appearances of truth to falsehood, and importance to trifles; but to teach them to weigh things in an impartial balance, and by the words of truth and soberness, to lead them into the paths of wisdom and goodness.

This is a satisfaction which I peculiarly find this day, while I am urging you to that religious care in the education of children, which I have at large opened in the former discourse. And it is a circumstance of additional pleasure, that I am pleading the cause of the weak and the helpless; of little tender creatures, who are incapable of pleading for themselves, and know not how much their interest is concerned. Nor am I without a secret hope, that if the divine spirit favour us with his assistance, some who are yet unborn may have eternal reason to rejoice in the fruits of what you are now to hear. Amen.

Having already endeavored to describe the way in which children are to be trained up; I now proceed,

Secondly, To propose some arguments to engage parents to this pious care.

And here I would intreat you distinctly to consider,—that the attempt itself is pleasant;—you have great reason to hope it may be successful;—and that success is of the highest importance.

I. The attempt itself is pleasant.

I speak not merely of the pleasure arising from the consciousness of discharging present duty, and a probable view of future success; such a satisfaction may attend those actions, which are in themselves most painful and mortifying. But I refer to the entertainment immediately flowing from the employment itself, when rightly managed. This is undoubtedly one of those ways of wisdom, which are ways of pleasantness, as well as a path, which in its consequences is peace and happiness: It is a commandment, in keeping of which there is a great reward.

The God of nature has wisely annexed a secret unutterable delight, to all our regular cares for the improvement of our rising offspring. We rejoice to see our tender plants flourish, to observe how the stock strengthens, and the blossoms and the leaves successively unfold. We trace with a gradually advancing pleasure, their easy smiles, the first efforts of speech on their stammering tongues, and the dawnings of reason in their feeble minds. It is a delightful office to cultivate and assist opening nature, to lead the young strangers into a new world, and to infuse the principles of any useful kind of knowledge which their age may admit, and their circumstances require. But when we attempt to raise their thoughts to the great Father of Spirits, to present them as in the arms of faith, to Jesus the compassionate shepherd, and teach them to enquire after him; when we endeavour to instruct them in the principles of divine truth, and form them to sentiments of prudence, integrity and generosity; we find a pleasure superior to what any other labour for their improvement can give.

On this occasion, my friends, I persuade myself, I may appeal to the repeated experience of many amongst you. Do you not find, that the sweetest truths of christianity, which are your hope and your joy in this house of your pilgrimage, are peculiarly sweet when you talk them over with your children? Do you not find, that your instructions and admonitions to them return into your own bosom with a rich increase of edification and refreshment? thus while you are watering these domestic plantations, you are watered also yourselves; and from these holy converses with your children, you rise to more endearing communion with your heavenly father: God by his spirit visiting your souls in the midst of those pious cares, and giving you immediate comfort and strength, as a token of his gracious acceptance, and perhaps as a pledge of future success. This leads me to urge the religious education of children.

II. By the probability there is, that it will be attended with such success, as to be the means of making them wise and good.

This is the argument urged by Solomon in the text, *Train up a child in the way in which he should go; and when he is old he will not depart from it.* Being early initiated into the right way, he will pursue it with increasing pleasure; so that with regard to the prosperity of the soul, as well as of the body, *his path will be like the morning light, which shineth more and more unto the perfect day.*

It is true, this assertion is to be understood with some limitation, as expressing the probability, rather than the certainty of the success; otherwise experience would contradict it in some melancholy instances. Would to God there were none untractable under the most pious and prudent methods of education; none, who *like deaf adders stop their ears* against *the voice of the* most skilful *charmers*, and have been accustomed to do it from their infancy! Would to God there were none of those, who appeared to *set out well*, and seemed eager. in *enquiring the way to Zion with their faces thitherward*, who have *forgotten the guides of their youth, and the covenant of their God*, and are to this day, wandering in the paths of the destroyer, if they are not already fallen in them! But do you throw by every medicine, which some have used without being recovered by it; or decline every profession of which there are some who do not thrive? What remedy must you then take? what calling must you then pursue? The application is obvious. It would be folly to pretend to maintain, that religious education will certainly obtain its end: but let me entreat you to consider,—that it is in its own nature a very rational method,—that it is the method which God has appointed, and a method which in many instances has been found successful. Attend seriously to these remarks, and then judge whether prudence and conscience will not oblige you to pursue it.

1. The relgious education of children is a very rational method of engaging them to walk in the way in which they should go.

There is the most evident advantage attending our early attempts of this kind, that we shall find the mind more open and disengaged, not tainted with all those corrupt principles, nor enslaved to those irregular habits, which they would probably imbibe and contract in the advance of age. Though the paper on which we would write the knowledge of God be not entirely fair, it is clear of many a foul inscription and deep blot, with which it would soon be covered. Though the garden, in which we would plant the fruits of holiness, be not free from weeds, yet many of them are but (as it were) in the invisible seed, and the rest are not grown up to that luxuriant size, which we must expect, if due cultivation be omitted or delayed.

It is a farther advantage which deserves to be mentioned here, that infancy and childhood is the most impressible age; and as principles are then most easily admitted, so they are most firmly retained. The ancients, those judicious observers of human nature, as well as many modern writers, are full of this remark in their discourses on education, and illustrate it by a great many beautiful allusions which are well known.

The new vessel takes a lasting tincture from the liquor which is first poured in: The soft clay is easily fashioned into what form you please; The young plant may be bent with a gentle hand; and the characters engraved on the tender bark, grow deeper and larger on the advancing tree. It will be our wisdom then to seize these golden opportunities and so much the rather, as it is certain they will either be improved or perverted; and that if they are not pressed into the service of religion, they will be employed as dangerous artillery against it.

But you will say, "With all these advantageous circumstances we cannot infuse grace into the hearts of our children; and after all our precautions, corrupt nature will prevent us and fix a wrong bias on the mind, before we can attempt to direct it aright." A mournful, but too evident truth! which, far from denying or suppressing, I would often declare and inculcate; and the rather now, as it greatly confirms my argument. Are the influence of a degenerate nature unavoidably so strong, and will you suffer them to be confirmed by these additional advantages? Do you apprehend, that, running with the footmen, you shall be in danger of fainting; and do you for that very reason chuse to contend with the horsemen; You cannot sure, in the face of so much reason and scripture, urge this as an excuse against making any attempts at all of this kind; and how then is it an apology for the neglect of those, which are (other things being equal,) the most rational and easy? But the trifling plea is more evidently silenced by observing,

2. The religious education of children is a method which God has appointed; and this greatly encreases the probability of its success.

I assuredly know, (and may God more deeply engrave it on our hearts!) that with regard to your labours as well as ours, *neither is he that planteth any thing, nor he that watereth, but God that giveth the increase.* But consider, I beseech you, how that increase is to be hoped for: Is it in the omission, or in the use of prescribed means? I urge it on your consciences, my friends, that religious education is an ordinance of God, which, therefore, you may reasonably hope, he will honour with a blessing. And you might as justly expect, that your souls should flourish in an unnecessary absence from the table and house of the Lord, or an habitual neglect of reading and prayer; as that your children should grow up for God, while you fail in your endeavours to engage them in his service. I repeat it again, religious education is an ordinance of God. And is it a work of labour and difficulty to prove the assertion? Which of you does not know; that christian parents, are solemnly charged to *bring up their children in the nurture and admonition of the Lord;* and that even under the Mosaic œconomy, God urged it on his people in a very affecting manner? Surely you must have observed, how strictly God charges it upon the Jews to take all opportunities to this purpose occasional as well as stated. *These words, says he, which I command thee this day, shall be in thine heart; and thou shalt teach them diligently to thy children, and shalt talk of them when thou sitest in thine house, and when thou walkest by the way, and when thou liest down, and when thou risest up.* And elsewhere, *thou shalt teach them to thy sons, and thy sons' sons.* Plainly recommending a care of remote, as well as immediate descendants of grand-children as well as children. Thus when God *established a testimony in Jacob, and appointed a law in Israel, he commanded the fathers, that they should make them known unto their children; that the generation to come might know them, even the children* that should be born, that they should arise and declare them to their children; that so religion might be transmitted to every rising age! You cannot be ignorant of such passages as these, which needs no coment to explain them, and consequently you cannot but know, that the religious education of children is a divine institution, as well as in itself a most rational attempt: After which you will not wonder to hear.

3. That it has in fact been attended with very happy success.

We acknowledge that the Great God does not confine himself to work by this way; and that he sometimes displays his sovereignty in visibly turning out of it. We acknowledge, that he sometimes leaves those who had been, as it were, born and brought up in his family, to forsake it in a very scandalous manner; while he seems to go into the territories of Satan, into ignorant, carnal, porfane families, and take from thence persons, whom he erects as trophies of free, surprising, and (as Mr. How justly expresses it) "unaccountable grace." But you well know, that these are more rare and uncommon cases; yet most of you, as I apprehend, were from your childhood trained up in the knowledge of God, and are living monuments of the success which has attended the care of parents, or masters in this particular. The greater part of those, who have of late been admitted to your communion, have to my certain knowledge, mentioned it with

D

thankfulness; and I rejoice to think, how many of the rising generation amongst us (if even a child may be known by his doings) are like to encrease the number, and give us an encouraging hope that they will at length be set as olive plants around the Lord's table, as well as yours. I persuade myself it is so elsewhere, and think I may pronounce it with some confidence, that the families of God's children are generally, speaking the nurseries of his church. Solomon, no doubt, had observed, that a good education had generally been successful, or we could by no means account for the remark in the text; and a very accurate writer of our own age and nation has carried it so far as to say, "that of all the men we meet with, nine parts in the ten are what they are, good or bad, useful or not, according to their education."

I hope you are by this time convinced, that, humanly speaking, there is great probability, that religious education may be the effectual means of promoting serious piety in the rising age; which was the second argument by which I was to recomend it: An argument, which may be greatly strengthened, by observing,

III. That the success, which we may so reasonably expect, is a matter of very high importance.

It is of evident importance—to the honour of God, and the support of religion.—to the present and future happiness of our children,

—and to your own comfort both in life and death. Weighty and comprehenfive tho'ts! which I fhall briefly touch, and to which I beg you will renew your attention.

1. The honour of God, and intereft of a Redeemer, is greatly concerned in the behaviour of your children; and confequently in your care of their education, which is like to have fo great an influence upon it.

We live in a dying world. Our fathers, where are they? Sleeping in the duft, as we muft fhortly be. We are fure, that in a little a very little while, thefe places muft know us no more: And when we are mouldering in the houfe of filence, who muft fill our places in the houfe of God! Who muft rife up in our ftead for the fupport of our religion amongft thofe that fucceed us? From whom can it be expected, but from our children? Yet how can we expect it from thefe, in the neglect of a method, which comes recommended by fo many advantageous circumftances? "Yes," you will perhaps be ready to fay, "God will take care of his own caufe, and Almighty grace will do what we have not attempted, becaufe we knew that we could not accomplifh it."—Almighty grace can indeed do it; and Almighty power can of thefe ftones, on which we tread raife up children to Abraham. But fhew me your warrant from the word of God for expecting it, either in the one cafe, or in the other.—You will poffibly anfwer, "He has promifed to be ever with his church and that the gates of Hell fhall not prevail against it; but that one generation shall arise and declare his mighty works unto another, and that the kingdom of his Son shall continue as long as the sun and moon endure." Blessed be his name for these encouraging promises, which shall, no doubt be accomplished. But where has he engaged that this kingdom shall always continue amongst us? Such passages as these will no more prove, that the gospel shall never be removed from Great-Britain, than they would once have proved, that it should never have been taken away from Pergamos or Thyatira, or any other of the Asian churches, which have so many ages ago been given up to desolation.

Now let me intreat you for a few moments, to dwell upon that thought; what if the gospel should be lost from among your descendants! what if in the age of these little ones, or the next that shall succeed to theirs, the house of the Lord should be forsaken, and his table abanboned? What if the ministry should be grown into disuse, or the servants of Christ in it should have nothing to do, but to bear a fruitless testimony against an unbelieving generation, till (when their hearts are broken with so sad an office) the gospel here die with them, and religion be burried in their graves? Is it a thought easily to be supported by a true Israelite, that the ark of the Lord should thus be lost, and God should write upon us Ichabod, the sad memorials of a departed glory!

It would surely be peculiarly melancholy, that religion should die in the hands of those who were the children of the kingdom. And were not yours so? In this respect, my friends permit me to say, that I am a witness among some of you. When you have offered your children to baptism, you have delivered them into my hands, with an express declaration of your sincere desire, that they might be devoted to God; and have received them again with a solemn charge and promise to bring them up for him, if their lives should be continued. And as for those of you who do not practise this institution, I doubt not, but many of you are equally faithful in dedicating your infant offspring to God. Is it not then reasonable to expect from both, that they should be brought up as a seed to serve him? And from whom may we hope it, if not from you? If you have experienced the power of divine grace upon your own souls, and tasted that the Lord is gracious, methinks it should awaken a holy zeal to spread the sweet favour of his name and word wherever you come: You should labour to the utmost for the advancement of his gospel amongst all your acquaintance, and even amongst strangers; how much more in your own families, amongst those whom you have from him, amongst those whom you have so solemnly given back to him.

2. The character of your children, and consequently your care in their education, is of the most evident importance, to their

present and future happiness.

I need not surely employ a great deal of time in proving the truth of the assertion. As christians you must undoubtedly own, that *godliness is profitable to all things, having the promise of the life which now is,* as well as *of that which is to come.* If your children, through the divine blessing on your holy care, become truly religious, they will not only be preserved from those follies and crimes which stain the honor, and ruin the substance of families, but they will secure a fair reputation; they will take the most probable method to make life truly comfortable; they will be entitled to the paternal care & blessing of God, and to crown all will be heirs of eternal glory with him; and what could your most prudent, faithful, tender love wish for them as a greater, or indeed a comparable good? On the other hand, if they prove vicious and profane (which in so degenerate an age it is very probable they may, if they have no religious principle to secure them) what can you expect but their in——y and misery in this world and their e——l destruction in the next?

One would imagine, that such considerations as these should very deeply impress the heart of a parent; and if they were alone should be sufficient to gain the cause. You, who have so tender a regard to all their temporal concerns: you, that rise early, and sit up late, that you may advance their fortunes, that you may furnish them with those dubious and and uncertain poſſeſſions, which may be bleſſings or curſes, as they are improved or abuſed; can you bear to think that they may be forever poor and miſerable? Surely it ſhould cut you to the heart to look on a child and reflect, "here is an heir of eternal miſery: Alas! what am I doing for him? Preparing an eſtate? Contriving for his preſent convenience or grandeur? Vain, wretched, prepoſterous care! which to uſe a very plain ſimile, is but like employing yourſelves in trimming and adorning its clothes, while the child itſelf were fallen into the fire, and would be in danger of being deſtroyed, if not immediately plucked out. Haſten to do it with an earneſtneſs anſwerable to the extremity of the caſe, and ſo much the rather as the danger is in part owing to you.

I will not ſay how far your perſonal miſtakes in conduct may have been a ſnare and a temptation to your children; nor can I pretend to determine it. But I am confident of this, that they have derived from your corrupt and degenerate nature. Through your veins, the original infection which tainted the firſt authors of our race, has flowed down to them. And is not this an affecting thought? and ought it not to quicken you to attempt their relief?

Dr. Tillotſon ſets this in a very moving light; "When a man has by treaſon tainted his blood, and forfeited his eſtate, with what grief and regret does he look on his children, and think of the injury he has done to them by his fault; and how solicitous is he before he dies to petition the king for favour to his children; how earnestly does he charge his friends to be careful of them, and kind to them!" We are those traitors. Our children have derived from us a tainted blood, a forfeited inheritance. How tenderly should we pity them! How solicitously should we exert ourselves to prevent their ruin! Mr. Flavel expresses the thought still more pathetically. "Should I bring the plague into my family, and live to see all my poor children lie dying by the walls of my house, if I had not the heart of a tyger, such a sight would melt my very soul." And surely, I may add, were there a sovereign antidote at hand, perhaps an antidote I had myself used, should I not direct them to it, and urge them to try it, I should be still more savage and criminal. The application is easy. The Lord deeply impress it on your souls, that your children may not die eternally of the malignant plague they have taken from you!

This is one consideration which should certainly add a great deal of weight to the argument I am now upon. I will conclude the head with the mention of another: I mean, the peculiar advantages which you their parents have for addressing yourselves to them. You, who have known them from their infancy, are best acquainted with their temper, and manner of thinking; you, who are daily with them, may watch the moſt tender moments, the moſt favorable opportunities of pleading with them: your melting affection for them, will ſuggeſt the moſt endearing ſentiments and words on ſuch occaſions: their obligations to you, and love for you will probably diſpoſe them to attend, and with the greater pleaſure to what you may ſay, or your authority over them, your power of correction, and a ſenſe of their dependance upon you in life, may prevent much of that oppoſition and contempt, which from perverſe tempers others might expect; eſpecially if they were not ſupported by your concurrence, in their attempts to inſtruct and reform your children.

On the whole, then, ſince your obligations and your encouragements to attempt the work are ſo peculiar, I may reaſonably hope you will allow its due weight to this ſecond conſideration that the character and conduct of your children, and conſequently your care in their education is of the higheſt imimportance to their preſent and future happineſs. I add once more,—

3. It is of great moment to your own comfort both in life and death.

Solomon often repeats the ſubſtance of that remark: *A wiſe ſon maketh a glad father: but a fooliſh ſon is an heavineſs to his mother.* And the juſtice of it in both its branches is very apparent. Let me engage you ſeriouſly to reflect upon it as a moſt awakening inducement, to the discharge of the important duty I am recommending.

If you have reason to hope that your labours are not vain, but that your children are become truly religious; it must greatly increase your satisfaction in them, that they are dear to you, not only in the bands of the flesh, but in those of the Lord. You will not only be secure of their dutiful and grateful behavior to you, but will have the pleasure of seeing them grow up in their different stations to prospects of usefulness in the church and in the world. Should Providence spare you to the advance of age, they will be a comfort and honor to your declining years. You will, as it were, enjoy a second youth in their vigour and usefulness; nay, a sense of their piety and goodness will undoubtedly be a reviving cordial to you in your dying moments. A delightful thought will it indeed be! "I am going to take my leave of the world, and my scene of service is over; but I leave those behind me, who will appear for God in my stead, and act perhaps with greater fidelity and zeal for the support of religion in a degenerate age. I leave my dear children destitute, indeed, of my counsel and help, perhaps in no abundant affluence of worldly enjoyments! but I leave them under the guardian care of my father, and their father, of my God, and their God. I must soon be separated from them, and the distance between us must soon be as great as between earth and heaven: But as

I leave them under the best guidance in the wilderness, so I have a joyful persuasion that they will soon follow me into the celestial Canaan. Yet a little while, and I and my dear offspring shall appear together before the throne of God; and I shall stand forth with transport and say, Behold, here am I, and the children which my God has graciously given me. Then will the blessedness on which I now enter, be multiplied upon me, by the sight of every child that has a share in it. Now, Lord, sufferest thou thy servant to depart in peace, since thou hast directed not only mine eyes, but theirs to thy salvation.

But if you see the dear little ones, grow up for the destroyer; if you see those, whose infant days have given you so many tender pleasures, and so many fond hopes, deviating from the paths of duty and happiness, how deeply will it pierce you! you, now look upon them with a soft complacency, and say, "These are they that shall comfort us under our labours and our sorrows." But alas! my friends! if this be the case, "These are they, that will increase your labours, and aggravate your sorrows: that will hasten upon you the infirmities of age, or crush you the faster under the weight of them, till they have brought down your hoary hairs with anguish to the grave." Little do they or you think how much agony and distress you may endure from what you will see, and what you will fear concerning them. How many slighted admonitions, how many deluded hopes, how many anxious days, how many restless nights will concur to make the evening of life gloomy! And at length, when God gives you a dismission from a world, which the folly and wickedness of your children has so long imbittered, how painful will the separation be, when you have the prospect of seeing them but once more, and that at the tribunal of God, where the best you can expect (in their present circumstance) is to rise up in judgment against them, and to bear an awful testimony which shall draw down upon them aggravated damnation!

And let me plainly tell you, that if in these last moments, conscience should also accuse you of the neglect of duty and testify that your own sorrow, and your children's ruin, is in part chargeable upon that it will be a dreadful ingredient in this bitter cup, and may greatly darken, if not entirely suppress those hopes with regard to yourselves, which alone could support you in this mournful scene. I am fully persuaded, that if you knew the weight with which these things will sit upon your mind, in the immediate views of the eternal world, you would not suffer every trifling difficulty, or little care, to deter you from the discharge of those duties, which are so necessary to prevent these galling reflections.

To conclude: Let me intreat you seriously to weigh the united force of those arguments, which I have now been urging to excite your diligence in this momentous care of training up your children in the way in which they should go. Consider how pleasant the attempt is: consider how fair a probability there is that it may prosper, as it is in itself a very rational method, as it is a method God has appointed, and a method which he has crowned with singular success :—Consider how important that success is, to the honour of God, and interest of religion, to the temporal and eternal happiness of your children, and finally, to your own comfort, both in life and death.

On the whole, I well know, and am persuaded, sirs, that you yourselves are convinced, that whatsoever can be opposed to such considerations as these, when laid in an impartial balance, it is altogether lighter than vanity. I do therefore seriously appeal to those convictions of your consciences as in the sight of God : And if from this time at least, the education of children amongst you be neglected, or regarded only as a light care, God is witness, and you yourselves are witnesses, that it is not for want of being plainly instructed in your duty, or seriously urged to the performance of it.

SERMON III.

ON THE EDUCATION OF CHILDREN.

PROV. XXII. 6.

Train up a Child in the way he should go; and when he is old he will not depart from it.

THOSE of you, who have made any observations on human life, must certainly know that if we desire to be agreeable and useful in it, we must regard not only the quality, but the manner of our actions; and that while we are in the pursuit of any important end, we must not only attend to those actions which do immediately refer to it, but must watch over the whole of our conduct; that we may preserve a consistency in the several parts of it. Otherwise we shall spoil the beauty and acceptance of many an honest, and perhaps in the main, prudent attempt; or by a train of unthought of consequences, shall demolish with the one hand, what we are labouring to build up with the other.

This is a remark which we shall have frequent occasion to recollect; and it is of peculiar importance in the business of education. It is therefore necessary, that having before described the way in which children are to be trained up, and urged you to a diligent application to the duty, I now proceed,

Thirdly, To offer some advices for your assistance in this attempt of leading children into, and conducting them in this way.

These will relate—partly to the manner in which the attempt is to be made,—and partly to the precautions necessary for rendering it effectual: Which are as you see, matters of distinct consideration, though comprehended under the general head of directions.

I. As to the manner in which the attempt is to be made.

And here it is evident it should be done plainly,—seriously,—tenderly, and patiently.

1. Children are to be instructed plainly: In the plainest things, and by the plainest words.

They are to be taught the plainest things in religion in the first place. And it is a pleasing reflection on this occasion, that according to the abundant goodness and condescension of the great God, those things which are the most necessary are the plainest. Just as in the world of nature, those kinds of food, which are most wholesome and nourishing, are also the most common. We should shew our grateful sense of the divine goodness in this particular, by our care to imitate it; and should see to it, that when the necessities of our children require bread, we do not give them a stone, or chaff; as we should do, if we were to distract their feeble minds with a variety of human schemes, and doubtful disputations. The more abstruse and mysterious truths of the gospel are gradually to be unfolded, as they are exhibited in the oracles of God, and to be taught in the language of the spirit; according to the excellent advice of the great Dr. Owen "making scripture phraseology our rule and pattern in the declaration of spiritual things." But we must not begin here. We must feed them with milk while they are babes, and reserve the strong meat for a maturer age. Take the obvious and vital truths of christianity. Tell them, that they are creatures, and sinful creatures; that by sin they have displeased a holy God; and that they must be pardoned, and sanctified, and accepted in Christ, or must perish forever. Shew them the difference between sin and holiness; between a state of nature and of grace. Shew them, that they are hastening on to death and judgment, and so must enter on heaven or hell, and dwell forever in the one or the other. Such kind of lessons will probably turn to the best account, both to them and you. I know it is a very easy thing to inflame the warm, ignorant minds of children with an eager zeal for distinguishing forms or distinguishing phrases; and to make them violent in the interest of a party, before they know any thing of common christianity. But if we thus sow the wind, we shall probably reap the whirlwind; venting ourselves, and transfusing into them, a wrath of man, which never works, but often greatly obstructs the righteousness of God. Blessed be God, this is not the fault of you my friends, of this congregation. I would mention it with great thankfulness, as both your happiness and mine, that so far as I can judge, it is the sincere milk of the word that you desire. Let it be your care to draw it out for the nourishment of your children's souls, as their understandings and capacities will permit them to take it in.

And while you are teaching them the plainest things, endeavor to do it in the plainest words. It is the gracious method which God uses with us, who speaks to us heavenly things in language, not fully expressive of the sublimity and grandeur of the subject, but rather suited to our feeble apprehensions. Thus our Lord taught his disciples, as they were able to bear it; and used easy and familiar similitudes, taken from the most obvious occurrences in life, to illustrate matters of the highest importance. A most instructive example! Such condescension should we use, in training up those committed to our care and should examine whether we take their understandings along with us, as we go on: Otherwise we are speaking in an unknown tongue, and as the Apostle expresses it, are barbarians unto them, be our language ever so grateful, elegant or pathetic.

Give me leave to add, for the conclusion of this head, that though it is to be taken for granted that children in their earliest infancy are to be engaged to what is good, and to be restrained from evil, chiefly by a view to rewards and punishments, more immediate or remote, or by some natural workings of a benevolent affection, which are by all means to be cherished and cultivated; yet as they may grow up to greater ripeness of understanding, something farther is to be attempted. It must then be our care, to set before them in the strongest light, the natural beauties of holiness, and deformities of sin; and likewise to propose, in the easiest and most familiar way the evidences of the truth of christianity, that they may be fortified against those temptations to infidelity, with which the present age does so unhappily abound. The external evidences of it are by no means to be slighted, such as the credibility of the gospel history, the accomplishment of prophecies, the unity of design carried on by so many different persons in distant ages and countries, its amazing and even miraculous propagations in the world; all which, with many other considerations to the same purpose, are very judiciously handled in a variety of excellent writings of our own age: of which I know not any more suited to your use than Mr. Bennet's discourses on the inspiration of scripture, which I therefore recommend to your attentive perusal, and with them Dr. Watts' sermons on the inward witness to the truth of christianity, from its efficacious tendency to promote holiness: This appears to me the noblest evidence of all, and will to those, who have actually experienced it, be an anchor of the soul both sure and stedfast.

2. *Children should be instructed in a very serious manner.*

There is an unhappy proneness in our degenerate natures to trifle with the things of God; and the giddiness of childhood is peculiarly subject to it. Great care should therefore be taken, that we do not encourage such a humour, nor teach them by our levity or indolence in the manner of our instruction, to take the awful name of God in vain, while they are speaking of him, or to him. For this purpose we must labour with our own hearts, to work them to a deep and serious sense of the truth and importance of what we say: This will give us an unaffected solemnity in speaking, which will probably command the attention, and impress the hearts of our children. Endeavour to preserve on your own spirit, an habitual awe of the great and blessed God, the Lord of heaven and earth: that when you speak of him to those little creatures they may evidently see the indications of the humblest veneration and reverence, and so may learn to fear him from their youth. When you speak of Christ, let your souls be bowing to him as the son of God, through whom alone you and yours can obtain pardon and life; and let them be overflowing with love to him, for his unutterable and inconceivable grace. And when you remind them of death judgement and eternity, consider yourselves and them as dying creatures: Think in how few months, or weeks, or days, your lips may be silent in the dust, or they may be forever removed beyond the reach of your instructions; and plead with them in as earnest and importunate a manner, as if the salvation of their immortal souls depended on the effect of the present address. Again,

3. Children should be instructed in a very tender and affectionate manner.

We should take care to let them see, that we do not desire to terrify and amaze them, to lead them into unnecessary severities, or to deprive them of any innocent pleasures; that what we say is not dictated by an ostentation of our wisdom and authority; but that it all proceeds from a hearty love to them, and an earnest desire of their happiness. Study therefore to address them in the most endearing language, as well as with the softest and sweetest arguments. Endeavour, according to the practice of Solomon, to find out acceptable words. And if tears should rise while you are speaking do not suppress them. There is a language in them, which may perhaps affect beyond words. A weeping parent is both an awful and a melting sight.

Endeavour therefore to look upon your children in such a view, as may be most likely to awaken these tender sentiments. Consider them as creatures, whom you (as instruments) have brought into being, tainted with innate corruption, surrounded with snares, and on the whole, in such apparent danger, that if not snatched as brands out of the burning, they must perish forever. And that your hearts may be further molified, and you may be formed to the most gentle and moving manner of address, let me intreat you to study the scripture in this view, and to observe the condescending and endearing forms in which the blessed God speaks to us there. Observe then for yourselves, and point them out to your children. Tell them, how kindly he has demanded, how graciously he has encouraged their services; while he says, *remember now thy creator in the days of thy youth;* and elsewhere, *I love them that love me, and those that seek me early shall find me.* Tell them that the Lord Jesus Christ hath invited them to come to him; for he has said, *Come unto me all ye that labour, and are heavy laden, and I will give you rest: Him that cometh unto me, I will in no wise cast out; And whosoever will, let him take of the water of life freely.* Such scriptures as these should often be repeated to them, and should be early inculcated on their memory, with an attempt, as far as possible, to let them into the spirit and force of them.

Nor will it be improper sometimes to set before them, how much you have done, how much you are ready to do for them; how many anxious thoughts you entertain, how many fervent prayers you offer on their account. Thus Lemuel's mother addressed him, *What, my son? and what, the son of my womb? and what, the son of my vows?* As if she had said, "My dear child, for whom I have borne so much, for whom I have prayed so earnestly; in what words shall I address thee, to express what my heart feels on thy account? How shall I speak my affectionate, overflowing concern for thy happiness both for time and eternity?" So Solomon pleads. *My son, if thine heart be wise, my heart shall rejoice, even mine:* As if he should say, "Think how much is comprehended in the argument, that a parent's happiness is in great measure to be determined by thy character and conduct." And the apostle Paul lays open his heart to the Gallatians in these prophetic words, *My little children of whom I travail in birth again, 'till Christ be formed in you.*

Yet these were, comparatively, strangers to him. And should not you, my friends, feel, should not you express, an equal tenderness for those who are so nearly allied to you in the bonds of nature, for those who are indeed parts of yourselves? But further,

4. Children should also be instructed patiently.

You know, when the husbandman has committed the seed to the ground, he patiently expects the fruit of his labours. So must ministers do when instructing their people: So must parents do, when instructing their children. You must not imagine, my friends, that a plentiful harvest will spring up in a day. The growth of nature is slow, and by insensible degrees: Nor are you to wonder, if advances in knowledge and grace be still slower. Be upon your guard therefore against fretfulness and impatience. Your children will forget what you have once taught them; repeat it a second time; and if they forget it the second time, repeat it the third. It is thus the great God deals with you, and you have daily reason to rejoice that he does. He knows the frailty and weakness of your minds, and therefore acts by a rule, which seems to be laid down with a peculiar regard to the very point I am urging : *whom shall he teach knowledge, and whom shall he make to understand doctrine ? them that are weaned from the milk, and drawn from the breasts? For precept must be upon precept, precept upon precept, and line upon line, line upon line ; here a little and there a little :* As if he should have said, " God has treated you like little children, who must have the same short, easy lesson repeated again and again." And is it not indeed thus with regard to you ? Does not the patience and condescension of your heavenly father send to you his ministers sabbath after sabbath, frequently inculcating the same things, that what you have forgot may be brought to mind again ? Thus should you do by those committed to your care.

Be teaching them every sabbath : That is remarkably a good day for the purpose. Then you have leisure for it ; then you have particular advantage to pursue the work ; then you are furnished with some new matter by what you have heard in public ; and

I would hope your spirits are then quickened by it, so that you can speak out of the abundance of your heart; and you may, by discoursing with them on what has been addressed to you, receive the impression on your own souls.

I add, Be teaching them every day, by occasional discourses, when you have not an opportunity of doing it by stated addresses. Drop a word for God every day and often in a day. You will probably find your account in it, and your children theirs. A sudden glance of thought towards God in the midst of the world, is often a great refreshment to the christian; and a sudden turn to something serious and spiritual in conversation, is frequently very edifying to others. It strikes the memory and the heart, and is perhaps, as a nail fixed in a sure place, when many a solemn admonition, and many an elaborate sermon is lost. It is with pleasure that I frequently hear good christians speaking of such occasional hints, which have been dropped by saints of the former generation: Those transient passages, which the pious parents might forget in a few moments, their children have distinctly remembered for many future years, and repeated for their own edification, and I might add for mine. Let this therefore be an encouragement to you; and in this respect, in the morning sow this precious seed, and in the evening withhold not your hand, since you know not whether shall prosper, or whether shall both be alike good.

Once more, let me intreat you to repeat your pious inſtructions and admonitions, even though your children ſhould grow up to years of maturity, without appearing to profit by them. Say not, that you can teach them no more than they readily know; or that you can try no new method which you have not already attempted. You ſee, that in our aſſemblies God often brings back ſouls to himſelf by ſetting home on the conſcience truths, which with regard to the ſpeculative part of them, they know as well as their teachers; and adds a divine efficacy to thoſe inſtitutions, which, for a long ſucceſſion of years, they had attended in vain. Be not therefore weary in well doing; but let patience in this inſtance, have its perfect work.

Thus let your children be inſtructed plainly, ſeriouſly, tenderly and patiently! I wave ſome other particulars, which might have added to theſe concerning the manner of inſtructing them, becauſe I apprehend they will fall under the ſecond branch of theſe directions: Where I am further to adviſe you,

II. As to the precautions you muſt uſe, if you deſire that theſe attempts in the religious education of your children may be attended with ſucceſs.

Here I would particularly adviſe,—that a prudent care be taken to keep up your authority over them, and at the ſame time, to engage their affections to you—that you be solicitous to keep them out of the way of temptation—that you confirm your admonitions by a suitable example—that you cheerfully accept of proper assistances in this important attempt—and that you humbly and constantly look up to God for his blessing on all.

1. If we desire to succeed in our attempts for the religious education of our children, we must take care to keep up our authority over them.

To this purpose, we must avoid, not only what is grossly vicious and criminal, (which will more properly be mentioned under a following head) but also those little levities and follies which might make us appear contemptible to them. Whatever liberties we may take with those who are our equals in age and station, a more exact decorum is to be preserved before our children. Thus we are to reverence them if we desire they should reverence us; for, as Dr. Tillotson very justly observes—" There is a certain freedom of conversation, which is only proper amongst equals in age and quality, which, if we use before our superiors, we seem to despise them, and if we do it before our inferiors, we teach them to despise us."

I will not insist on this hint, which your own prudence must accommodate to particular circumstances; but shall here introduce the mention of correction, which in some cases, may be absolutely necessary to the support of parental authority, especially where admonitions and counsels are slighted.

You know that the scriptures expresly require it on proper occasions; and Solomon in particular enlarges on the head, and suggests some important thoughts with regard to it.—Foolishness (says he) is bound up in the heart of a child, but the rod of correction shall drive it far from him. Nay, he speaks of it as a matter in which life is concerned, nay, even the life of the soul; *Withhold not correction from a child; for if thou beat him with a rod, he shall not die: Thou shalt beat him with a rod, and shalt deliver his soul from hell.* And is it kindness or cruelty in a parent to spare the flesh to the hazard of the soul? Parents are therefore exhorted to an early care in this respect, lest vicious habits growing inveterate, should render the attempt vain or hurtful; and they are cautioned against that foolish tenderness which leads them to regard the tears of a child rather than its truest and highest interest.—*Correct thy son while there is hope, and let not thy soul spare for his crying: he that spareth the rod, hateth his son; but he that loveth him, chasteneth him betimes.* Nor can we imagine a more lively commentary on the words than the melancholy story of Eli, who, though he was a very eminent saint in a degenerate age, yet erred here, and by a fatal indulgence, brought ruin, as well as infamy on himself and family. He reproved the abominable wickedness of his sons; but did not make use of those severe methods which in such a case, the authority of a parent might have warranted, and the office of a judge did undoubtedly require. Observe the sentence which God pronounced against him for it, and which he executed upon him in a very awful manner. The Lord said unto Samuel, Behold, I will do a thing in Israel, at which both the ears of every one that heareth it shall tingle: In that day I will perform against Eli all things which I have spoken concerning his house; when I begin I will also make an end, For I have told him that I will judge his house forever, for the iniquity which he knoweth; because his sons made themselves vile, and he restrained them not: And therefore, I have sworn unto the house of Eli, that the iniquity of Eli's house shall not be purged with sacrifice nor offering forever. Take heed, I entreat you, as you love your children, as you love yourselves, that it may not be said of you, that yours have made themselves vile, and you have neglected to restrain them. Let mothers, in particular, take heed that they do not, as it were, smother their children in their embraces, as a French author expresses it. And let me remind you all particularly to be cautious that the arms of one parent be not a refuge from the resentment of the other. Both should appear to act in concert, or the authority of the one will be despised, and probably the indulgence of the other abused, and the mutual affection of both endangered.

I cannot say, that I enlarge on this subject with pleasure; but how could I have answered for the omission of what is so copiously, and so pathetically inculcated in the sacred writings? It is indeed probable that the rugged and servile temper of the generality of the Jewish nation, might render a severe discipline peculiarly necessary for their children; yet I fear, there are few of our families, where every thing of this kind can safely be neglected. But after all, I would by no means drive matters to extremities; and therefore cannot persuade myself to dismiss the head without a caution or two. Take heed, that your corrections be not too frequent; or too severe, and that they be not given in an unbecoming manner.

If your corrections be too frequent, it will probably spoil much of the success. Your children, like iron, will harden under repeated strokes; and that ingenious shame will be gradually worn off, which adds the greatest sting to what they suffer from a parent's hand. And there will be this farther inconvenience attending it, that there will not be a due difference made, between great and small faults. The laws of Draco the Athenian, were justly rejected, because they punished all crimes alike, and made the stealing of an apple capital, as well as the murther of a citizen. You, on the contrary, should let your children see, that you know how to distinguish between indiscretion and wickedness; and should yourselves appear most displeased, where you have reason to believe God is so.

Nor should your corrections at any time be too severe. It is prettily said by Dr. Tillotson on this occasion, "that whips are not the cords of a man: They should be used in family, only (as the sword in the republic) as the last remedy when all others have been tried in vain; and then should be so used, as that we may appear to imitate the compassion of our heavenly father, who doth not afflict willingly, nor grieve the children of men."

Which leads me to add, that we should be greatly cautious, that correction be not inflicted in an unbecoming manner; and it always is so, when it is given in a passion. A parent's correcting his child should be regarded as an act of domestic justice, which therefore should be administered with a due solemnity and decorum; and to behave otherwise on the occasion, is almost as great an indecency, as for a judge to pass sentence in a rage. It is injurious to ourselves, as it tends to spoil our own temper; for peevishness and passion will grow upon us, by being indulged towards those who dare not oppose them: And it is on many accounts injurious to our children. Solomon intimates, that correction and instruction should be joined, when he says, *The rod and reproof give wisdom.* But what room is there for the still voice of wisdom to be heard in a storm of fury? If your children see, that you act calmly and mildly; if they read parental tenderness in your heart, through an awful frown on your brow; if they perceive that correction is your strange work, a violence which you offer to yourselves from a principle of duty to God and affection to them; they must be obdurate indeed, if they do not receive it with reverence and love; for this is both a venerable and an amiable character. But if once they imagine, that you chastise them merely to vent your passion, and gratify your resentment, they will secretly despise, and perhaps hate you for it: In that instance at least, they will look upon you as their enemies, and may, by a continued course of such severities, contract such an aversion, not only to you, but to all that you recommend to them. Thus you may lose your authority and your influence, by the very method you take to support it, and may turn a wholesome, though bitter medicine into poison. But I hope and trust, that your humanity and your prudence will concur to prevent so fatal an abuse.

2. If you desire success in your attempts for the education of your children, you must be careful to secure their affection to you.

Our Lord observes, that if any man love him he will keep his word; and the assertion is applicable to the present case: The more you children love you, the more will they regard your instructions and admonitions. God has indeed made it their duty to love you, and the most indispensable laws of gratitude require it; yet since so many children are evidently wanting in filial affection, it is certain that all this may not secure it in yours, unless you add a tender, obliging behaviour to all the other benefits you have conferred upon them. I observed under a former head, that you should address them in an affectionate manner when discoursing on religious subjects; but now I add, that you should carry the temper through life, and be daily endeavoring to render yourselves amiable to them. The Apostle cautions parents that they should not provoke their children to wrath, if they would bring them up in the nurture and admonition of the Lord: On the contrary, you should put on the kindest looks, you should use the most endearing and condescending language; you should overlook many little failings, and express a high complacency in what is really regular and laudable in their behaviour. And though you must sometimes over-rule their desires, when impatiently eager, yet far from delighting generally to cross them, you should rather study their inclinations, that you may surprize them with unexpected favours. Thus will they learn quietly to refer themselves to your care, and will more easily submit to mortification and denial, when it is not made necessary by clamourous and impetuous demands. On the whole, you should endeavour to behave so, as that your children may love your company, and of choice be much in it; which will preserve them from innumerable snares, and may furnish you with many opportunities of forming their temper and behaviour, by imperceptible degrees, to what may be decent, amiable and excellent.

If you manage these things with prudence, you need not fear that such condescentions, as I have now recommended will impair your authority; far from that, they will rather establish it. The superiority of your parental character may be maintained in the midst of these indulgencies; and when it is thus attempered, it is most like to produce that mixture of reverence and love, by which the obedience of a child is to be distinguished from that of a slave.

3. You must be solicitous to keep your children out of the way of temptation, if you would see the success of your care in their education.

If you are not on your guard here, you will probably throw down what you have built, and build up that which you have been endeavoring to destroy. An early care must be taken to keep them from the occasions, and the very appearances of evil. We would not venture their infant steps on the brink of a prescipice on which grown persons, who know how to adjust the poise of their bodies, may walk without extreme danger. More hazardous might it be to allow them to trifle with temptations, and boldly to venture to the utmost limits of that which is lawful. An early tenderness of conscience may be a great preservative;

and the excess of strictness (though no excess be desirable) may prove much safer than an excess of liberty.

Bad company is undoubtedly one of the most formidable and pernicious entanglements. By forming friendships with persons of a vicious character, many a hopeful youth has learnt their ways, and found a fatal snare to his soul. You should be very watchful to prevent their contracting such dangerous friendships; and where you discover any thing of that kind, should endeavour, by all gentle and endearing methods, to draw them off from them; but if they still persist, you must resolve to cut the knot you cannot untie, and let your children know they must either renounce their associates, or their parents. One resolute step of this kind might have prevented the ruin of multitudes, who have fallen a sacrifice to the importunities of wicked companions, and the weak indulgence of imprudent parents; who have contented themselves with blaming, what they ought strenuously to have redressed.

All bad company is, in this respect, formidable; but that is most evidently so which is to be found at home. Great care ought therefore to be taken that you admit none into your families who may debauch the tender minds of your children, by pernicious opinions, or by vicious practices. This is a caution which should be particularly remembered in the case of servants. Take heed you do not bring into your families, such as may diffuse infection through the souls of your dear offspring. It is a thousand times better to put up with some inconveniences and disadvantages, when you have reason to believe a servant fears God, and will, from a principle of conscience be faithful in watching over your children, and in seconding your religious care in their education, than to prefer such, as while they are, perhaps, managing your temporal affairs something better, may pervert your children to the service of the devil. I fear some parents little think, how much secret mischief these base creatures are doing. And it is very possible, that if some of you recollect what you may have observed among the companions of your childhood, you may find instances of this nature, which riper years have not since given you opportunity to discover. See to it therefore, that you be diligently on your guard here.

Again: If you send your children to places of education, be greatly cautious in your choice of them. Dearly will you purchase the greatest advantages for learning, at the expence of those of a religious nature. And I will turn out of my way to add, that schoolmasters and tutors will have a dreadful account to give, if they are not faithfully and tenderly solicitous for the souls of those committed to their care. The Lord pardon our many defects here, and quicken us to greater diligence and zeal!—But to return:

Give me leave only to add, that it is of the highest importance if you would not have all your labour in the education of your children lost, that you should be greatly cautious with regard to their settlement in the world. Apprenticeships and marriages, into irreligious families, have been the known sources of innumerable evils. They who have exposed the souls of their children to apparent danger, for the sake of some secular advantages, have often lived to see them drawn aside to practices ruinous to their temporal as well as their eternal interest. Thus their own iniquity has remarkably corrected them: and I heartily pray, that the God of this world may never be permitted thus to blind your eyes: but that you, my friends, may learn from the calamities of other families, that wholesome lesson, which, if you neglect it, others may perhaps hereafter learn from the ruin of yours.

4. See to it, that you confirm your admonitions by a suitable example, if you desire on the whole that they should prove useful to your children.

A consciousness of the irregularity of our own behaviour, in any remarkable instances which may fall under their observation, will probably abate much of that force and authority with which we might otherwise address them. When we know they may justly retort upon us, at least in their minds, those words of the apostle, Thou that teachest another, teachest thou not thyself? Surely, a sense of guilt and of shame must either entirely silence us, or at least impair that freedom and confidence, with which we might otherwise have exhorted or rebuked.

Or had we so much composure and assurance, as to put on all the forms of innocence and virtue, could we expect regard, when our actions contradicted our discourses, or hope they should reverence instructions which their teachers themselves appear to despise? It is in the general true, that there is a silent but powerful oratory in example, beyond the force of the most elegant and expressive words; and the example of parents has often a particular weight with their children; which seems to be alluded to in that exhortation of St. Paul. *Be ye followers* (or imitators) *of God, as dear children.* So that on the whole, as a very celebrated writer well expresses it, "To give children good instruction, and a bad example, is but beckoning to them with the hand to shew them the way to Heaven, while we take them by the hand, and lead them in the way to Hell." We should therefore most heartily concur in David's resolution, as ever we hope our families should be religious and happy: *I will behave myself wisely in a perfect way: I will walk within my house with a perfect heart.*

5. Cheerfully accept of all proper assistances in the education of your children, if you desire it may succeed well.

It will be your wisdom to accept of the

assistance, which may be offered, either from books or friends.

Books may in this respect be very useful to you; the book of God, above all; both to furnish you with materials for this great work, and to instruct you in the manner of performing it. Other writings may be subservient to this purpose. Wise and pious treatises on the subject of education may be read with great pleasure and advantage; and you may receive singular assistance from those catechisms and prayers, and songs for children, with which most of your families are now furnished, through the condescension of one valuable friend in writing them & the generosity of another in bestowing them upon us. I hope you will express your thankfulness to both, by a diligent care to use them; and I persuade myself, that you and yours may abundantly find your account in them: for while the language is so plain and easy, that even an infant may understand it, you will often find not only a propriety, but a strength and sublimity in the sentiments, which may be improving to persons of advanced capacities. There is much of that milk, by which strong men may be entertained and nourished.

I add, that in this important work you should gladly embrace the assistance of pious and prudent friends. I can by no means approve that Lacedemonian law, which gave every citizen a power of correcting his neighbour's children, and made it infamous for the parent to complain of it: yet we must allow, that considering the great importance of education, a concern for the happiness of families and the public, will require a mutual watchfulness over each other in this respect: Nor is there any imaginable reason to exclude this from the number of those heads on which we are to admonish one another, and to consider each other to provoke unto good works.

Nothing seems more evident than this; and one would suppose, that persons, who are acquainted with human nature, should suspect that self love might work under this form, and that they might be a little blinded by a partial affection to their offspring. Such a reflection might engage them at least patiently, or rather thankfully, to hear the sentiments, and receive the admonitions of their friends on this head. But instead of this, there is in many people, a kind of parental pride, (if I may be allowed the expression) which seldom fails to exert itself on such an occasion. They are so confident in their own way, and do so majesterially despise the opinion of others, that one would almost imagine, they took it for granted that with every child, nature had given to the parent a certain stock of infallible wisdom for the management of it; or that, if they thought otherwise, they rather chose that their children should be ruined by their own conduct than saved by any foreign advice. If this arrogance only rendered the parents ridiculous, one should not need to be greatly concerned about it, especially as their high complacency in themselves would make them easy, whatever others might think or say of them: But when we consider the unhappy consequences it may produce, with regard to the temper and conduct of the rising generation, it will appear a very serious evil, well worthy a particular mention, and a particular care to guard against it.

As for the assistance of ministers in this work of education, I persuade myself you will be so wise as thankfully to embrace it, both in public and private; and let me urge you to improve it to the utmost. Accustom your children to an early constancy and seriousness in attending divine ordinances, and be often yourselves enquiring, and give us leave sometimes to enquire, how they advance in acquaintance with religion, and in love to it. And more particularly let them attend on our catechetical lectures which are peculiarly intended for their service.

I bless God, I have seen the happy effects of this exercise, both in the places where I was educated whilst a child, and in those where I was formerly fixed; and as I am now introducing it amongst you, with an intent to continue it as long as I am capable of public service, I promise myself your most hearty concurrence in it. I will not at large insist on the advantages which may attend it. You easily see, that it will be an engagement to the children to learn those excellent summaries of divine truth, when their progress in them is so often examined: By repeating it themselves, and hearing it rehearsed by others, it will be more deeply fixed upon their memories: The exposition of it in a plain and familiar manner may much improve their understandings in the doctrines and duties of religion: And I will add, you that are parents may, by attending on these occasions, possibly learn something as to the way of opening and explaining things, which you may successfully practise at home. In consequence of all we may hope, that by the divine blessing, some good impressions may be made on the minds of children. And when they find a minister willing to take pains to instruct them, when they hear him seriously and tenderly pleading with them, and pleading with God for them, it may much engage their affections to him, and so promote his usefulness amongst them, in other ordinances and in future years. And give me leave to say upon this head, that as no wise and good minister will think it beneath him, to desire the affection of the children of his congregation; so it is the duty of parents to cherish in their offspring, sentiments of respect and love to all the faithful ministers of Christ, and especially towards those who statedly labour amongst them. Whatever mistakes you may discover in our conduct, or whatever deficiencies in our public ministrations, you should study to conceal them from the notice of your children; lest they should grow up in a contempt of those, whose services might otherwise be highly advantageous to them.

6. Lastly, Be earnest in prayer to God for his blessing on your attempts in the education of your children, if you desire to see them successful.

This I would leave with you as my last advice ; and though I have had frequent occasion to hint at it before, I would now more particularly urge it on your attentive regard. God is the author of every good and every perfect gift ; it is he that has formed the mind and tongue, and that teaches man knowledge and address. On him therefore must you fix your dependence, to teach you so to conceive of divine things, and so to express your conceptions of them, as may be most suited to the capacities, the dispositions, and the circumstances of your children; and to him you must look to teach them to profit by all, by his almighty grace to open their ear unto discipline, and to bow their heart unto understanding.

A heathen poet could teach the Romans in a form of public and solemn devotion, to look up to Heaven for influences from thence, to form their youth to the love and practice of virtue. Surely you, my friends, are under much greater obligations to do it, and that in a christian manner; earnestly intreating the God of grace, to send down on your rising offspring the effusions of that blessed spirit, which was purchased by the blood of Christ, and is deposited in his compaſſionate hand. If you have taſted that the Lord is gracious, you are daily living on thoſe ſupplies; let it be your conſtant errand at the throne of grace to plead for your children there. Wreſtle with God in ſecret for the life of their ſouls, and for thoſe regenerating influences on which it depends; and in thoſe family devotions, which I hope you dare not neglect, let the little ones, from their earlieſt infancy, have a ſhare in your remembrance. You may humbly hope that He, by whoſe encouragement and command you pray, will not ſuffer theſe ſupplications to be like water ſpilt upon the ground: And in the nature of things, it may tend to make ſerious impreſſions on the minds of your children to hear their own caſe mentioned in prayer, and may diſpoſe them with greater regard to attend on what you ſay to them, when they find you ſo frequently, ſo ſolemnly, and ſo tenderly pleading with God for them.

Doubt not that every faithful miniſter of Chriſt will moſt heartily concur with you in ſo great and neceſſary a requeſt. May God return to our united addreſſes an anſwer of peace! May he *pour out his ſpirit on our ſeed, and his bleſſing on our offspring, that they may grow up before him as willows by the water courſes; that they may be to their parents for a comfort, to the church for a ſupport, and to our God for a name and a praiſe!* AMEN.

ON THE EDUCATION OF CHILDREN.

PROV. XXII. 6.

Train up a Child in the way he should go; and when he is old he will not depart from it.

IN treating on this subject of education, I have all along endeavored, according to my usual manner, to make my discourses as practical as I could. While I was describing and recommending the way, and offering my advices, with regard to the manner of conducting children into it, most of what I said under those generals was an application to you. I have therefore left myself the less to do here; yet I was not willing to conclude my discourses on a subject, which it is probable I shall never so largely resume, without

Fourthly, A particular address to my hearers, according to your different relations and characters in life.

This I promised as my fourth and last general, and I enter on it without farther preface: humbly begging that God, who has so intimate an access to all our hearts, would enable me to speak in the most awakening and edifying manner, and that he would, by his blessed spirit apply it to your consciences

that it may be as a nail faftened in a fure
place; that hearing and knowing thefe things
for yourfelves, you may hear and know
them for your good.

I would here particularly addrefs myfelf,
—firſt to parents, then to children, and—in
the laſt place to thoſe young perſons who
are grown up to years of maturity, but not
yet fixed in families of their own.

I. Let me addreſs my difcourfe to thofe
of you that are parents; whether you have
been negligent of the duties I have now been
urging, or through grace have been careful
in the difcharge of them.

1. To thoſe who have been groſsly negligent in this important care.

I have here one advantage not common
to every fubjeƈt; I mean that the guilty will
immediately know themſelves. When we
apply ourfelves in general to unconvert-
ed ſinners, ignorance of the nature of true
religion, a negleƈt of converfing with your
own fouls, or the infinuating prejudices of
felf love, may difguife the true ſtates of
the cafe, and teach people to fpeak peace
to themſelves, under the moſt awful denun-
ciations of wrath and vengeance. But here
one would imagine, that the recolleƈtion of
a few moments might be fufficient to determine the cafe; becaufe the queftion relates
to paſt faƈts, and not merely to one particular aƈtion, but to a long train, and fucceffion
of labours and attempts.

Now let your consciences witness whether I am guilty of a breach of charity, when I take it for granted that there are some amongst you, who have been, and are very negligent of the duty I have now been enforcing? You have probably contented yourselves with teaching your children to read, and setting them to learn, like parrots, a prayer, and perhaps too a catechism and a creed. But I appeal to your consciences—have you from the very day of their birth to this time ever spent one hour in seriously instructing them in the knowledge of God, and endeavoring to form them to his fear and service: in setting before them the misery of their natural condition, and urging them to apply to Christ for salvation: in representing the solemnities of death and judgment, and the eternal world, and urging an immediate and diligent preparation for them? Where is the time, where the place that can witness, that you have been pouring out souls before God on their account, and wrestling with him for their lives, as knowing they must perish forever without the righteousness of his Son, and the grace of his Spirit? Where or when have you thus prayed with them or for them? What sermon have you heard, what scripture have you read, with this thought, "This will I carry to my children, and communicate to them as the food of their souls?" I fear, there are several of you that have been so far from doing it, that you have hardly ever seriously thought of it as a thing to be done.

And I would ask, why have you not thought of it, and why have you not done it? Are these creatures, that you have produced like the other animals of your houses or your field, mere animated systems of flesh and blood, made to take a turn in life for a few days and months, and then to sink into everlasting forgetfulness? Or are they rational and immortal creatures, that must exist forever in Heaven or in Hell? This is not a matter of doubt with you; and yet you behave as if the very contrary to what you believe were evident certain truth. In short, it is the most barbarous part you act, and more like that of an enemy than a parent.

It is not that you are insensible of the workings of parental tenderness. No, far from that, it may perhaps sometimes rise to a weak and criminal dotage; yet I repeat it again, you are acting a hostile and barbarous part. You are greatly solicitous for their temporal happiness. For this you labour and watch; for this you deny yourselves many an enjoyment, and subject yourselves to many an uneasy circumstance: But, alas! Sirs, where is the real friendship of all this, while the precious soul is neglected? Your children are born with a corrupted nature, perverted by sinful examples, ignorant of God in a state of growing enmity to him, and in consequence of all, exposed to his wrath and curse, and in the way to everlasting ruin: In the mean time it is your great care, that they may pass through this precarious, momentary life, in ease and pleasure, perhaps in abundance and grandeur; that is, in such circumstances, as will probably lull them into a forgetfulness of their danger, till their be no more hope. How cruel a kindness!

It brings to my mind the account which an ancient writer gives of the old Carthagenians, which I can never recollect without great emotion. He is speaking of that diabolical custom which so long prevailed amogst them, of offering their children to a detestable idol, which was formed in such a manner, that an infant put into his hands, which were stretched out to receive it, would immediately fall into a gulf of fire. He adds a circumstance, which one cannot mention without horror; that the mothers, who with their own hands presented the little innocents, thought it an unfortunate omen that the victim should be offered weeping; and therefore used a great many fond artifices to divert it, that soothed by the kisses and caresses of a parent, it might smile in the dreadful moment in which it was to be given to the idol. Pardon me, my friends; such is your parental care and love; such your concern for the present ease and prosperity of your children, while their souls are neglected: A fond solicitude, that they may pass smiling into the hands of the destroyer!

You know, with what just severity God reckons with the Israelites for their abominable wickedness, in taking his sons and his daughters, for so he calls the children of his professing people, and sacrificing them to be devoured: And can you suppose, he will take no notice of the unnatural neglect of yours. Not to endeavor to save, is to destroy; and is it a little guilt, when an immortal soul is in question? You probably remember those terrible words in Ezekiel; (may they be deeply inscribed on the hearts of all whom they concern!) *Son of man, I have made thee a watchman to the house of Israel, therefore hear thou the word from my mouth, and give them warning from me;—and if thou speakest not to warn the wicked from his wicked way, to save his life, the same wicked man shall die in his iniquity, but his blood will I require at thine hand.* If ever you read this passage with attention, you must own it is exceedingly awful, and must be ready to say, " The Lord be merciful to ministers! they have a solemn account to give." Indeed they have; and we thank you, if you ever bestow a compassionate thought and prayer upon us. But permit me to remind you, and though it be our case, it is not ours alone; you have likewise your share in it. Your children are much more immediately committed to your care, than you and they are committed to ours; and, by all parity of reason, if they perish in their iniquities, while you neglect to give them warning, their blood will be required at your hand.

And when God comes to make inquisition for that blood, how will you be able to endure it? That awful day will open upon you, and the tribunal of God, in all its terrors, will stand unveiled before you. Give me leave to direct your eyes to it in this distant prospect, while there is yet room to mitigate those terrors. If you go on in this cruel negligence of the souls of your children, how will you dare to meet them at that judgment seat? How will you be able to answer the great Father of Spirits, when expostulating with you on account of his offspring, as well as yours, who have been betrayed and ruined by your neglect? " Inhuman creatures," (may He justly say) to whom should I have committed the care of them rather than to you? Did they not, by my appointment, derive their being from you? Did I not implant in your hearts the natural affections of parents towards them? And to increase the obligation, did they ⬛ pass through the tender scenes of infancy and childhood in your arms and under your eye? If you had no compassion for their perishing souls, if you would exert no efforts for their deliverance and salvation, from whom could those compassions, those efforts have been expected? But wherein did they appear? Behold the book of my remembrance, the records of thy life, thrown open before thee: Where is the memorial of one hour spent in instruction, or in fervent prayer with them, or for them? Can I approve, can I acquit you on such a review? Or shall I not rather visit for these things, and shall not my soul be avenged for such a conduct as this?

And your children—will they be silent on the occasion? Did Adam, in the distress and amazement of his foul, when in the prefence of his judge, accufe Eve his wife, fo lately taken from his fide, and committed to his protection, and ftill, no doubt, appearing lovely in the midſt of forrow? and will your children in that terrible day fpare you? You may rather expect they will labor to the utmoſt to aggravate a crime which cofts them fo dear, that fo they may, if poffible, alleviate their own guilt, or if not indulge their revenge. "O God," (may they perhaps cry out in the moft piercing accents of indignation and defpair) "thou art righteous in the fentence thou paffeft upon us, and we juftly die for our iniquity. We have deftroyed ourfelves. But wilt thou not remember that our ruin is in part chargeable here? Had thefe our parents been faithful to thee and to us, it had perhaps been prevented. Had our infancy been formed by religious inftruction, we might not have grown up to wickednefs; we might not, in the advance of life, have defpifed thy word, and trampled on thy fon; but might this day have been owned by thee as thy children, and have rifen to that inheritance of light and glory, which we now behold at this unapproachable diftance. Oh! curfed be the fathers that begat us; curfed the wombs that bare us; curfed the paps that gave us fuck! remember us, O Lord, whilft thou art judging them, and let us have this one wretched comfort, in the midſt of all our agonies, that it is not with impunity that they have betrayed our souls!"

This indeed is shocking and diabolical language; and so for that very reason, it is so much the more probable on so dreadful an occasion. And give me leave to ask you one question, my friends, and I will conclude the head. If your children were crying out against you in the bitterness of their souls, could you attempt to silence them by reminding them of the care which you took of their temporal affairs, or of the riches and grandeur in which you left them on earth? Nay, could you have a heart so much as to mention such a trifle? And if you could not, then, in the name of God, sirs, how do you satisfy yourselves to confine all your thoughts and labours to that which, by your own confession, will neither secure your children from everlasting destruction, nor give them one moment's relief in the review when they are falling into it?

I will make no apology for the plainness, and earnestness, which I have used. Eternal interests are at stake, and the whole tenour of scripture supports me in what I say. I had rather you should be alarmed with hearing these things from me now, than tormented with hearing them in another manner from your children, and from God at last. If you please to take proper measures for preventing the danger, I have told you the way at large: If you do not, I hope I may say, "I am in this respect, clear from your blood, and the blood of yours, who may perish by your means: Look you to it."

But it is high time that I proceed in my address, and apply myself,

2. To those parents, who have been careful to discharge the duty, we have so copiously described and enforced.

I cannot suppose, that any of us would pretend to maintain, that in this, or any other branch of duty, we have acted up to the utmost extent and perfection of our rule. I hope an humble sense of the deficiences of all the best of our services, is frequently leading us to the believing views of a better righteousness than our own, in which alone we can dare to appear before a holy God, and answer the demands of his perfect law. Nevertheless, it is surely allowable to rejoice in the testimony of our conscience, with regard to the regularity of our own behaviour, so far as it is conformable to reason and scripture; and it is an important duty, thankfully to own those influences of sanctifying and strengthening grace, by which we are what we are.

It is with great pleasure I recollect the reason I have to believe, that many of you, christians, who hear me this day, are in the main conscienciously practising these duties;

More especially have you reason to adore it, if through grace you can say, with regard to the present success, what you may certainly say, as to the future recompense, that your labour in the Lord is not in vain. Let God have the glory of his own work. I persuade myself, you understand the gospel too well, to ascribe it to the prudence of your own conduct, to the strength of your reasoning, or to the warmth and tenderness of your address. Whatever of these advantages you have possessed, were derived from God; and your very care for your offspring, is, as the apostle expresses it in a like case, the earnest care which God has put into your hearts. But it was not this care, or these advantages alone, that produced so happy an effect. In vain had your doctrine from day to day dropped as the rain, and distilled as the dew, in the most gentle, and insinuating mannner; in vain had the precious seed of the word been sown with unwearied diligence, and watered with tears too; had not God commanded the operations of his blessed spirit to come down, as a more efficacious rain, as more fruitful showers to water their hearts. Oh! be not insensible of the favour. Your own souls might to this day, have been a barren wilderness, a land of drought, an habitation of devils; and behold, not only they, but your families too, are like a field, like a garden, which the Lord has blessed. God might have cut you off many years ago, for your neglect of his covenant, or your breaches of it; and behold he is establishing it, not only with you, but your seed after you, for an everlasting covenant. Methinks your hearts should overflow with gratitude and holy joy, while you dwell on such reflections as these. This should add a relish to all the pleasure you find in conversing with your children: This should quicken you to a farther diligence in cultivating those graces, which you have the satisfaction to see already implanted: This should reconcile you to all the afflictions, with which Providence may exercise, either you or them: This should support you in the views of a separation, either by our own death, or by theirs; since you have so comfortable a hope, that if they are removed they will go to a heavenly father, and that if they are left behind you, they will be safe and happy under his care, till you meet in a better world, where you will be forever to each other a mutual glory and joy.

But I cannot congratulate you on this occasion, without the danger of adding affliction to the afflicted parents, whose circumstances, alas! are far different from yours. I fear, my friends, that there are some amongst you, who look round you, and look forward, with far different prospects; some who are with bleeding hearts, borrowing the complaint, devoted to God in baptism, which we endeavoured to educate in the knowledge and fear of the Lord, the children of our hopes, the children of our prayers, are unfruitful unto all our cultivation, or, it may be, visibly turned aside from the good ways in which they were trained up; as if they had known them only to reject and affront them: So that we have reason to fear, that all we have done, as it is an aggravation of their guilt, will be a proportionable aggravation of their ruin."

It is indeed a very pitiable case. We owe you our compassions, and we owe you our prayers; but permit us to intermix our consolations and our admonitions. You have at least delivered your own souls; and as you participate in the sorrows of faithful ministers, you may share in their comfort too; and say with them, though the objects of our compassionate care be not gathered, yet shall we be glorified, for our work is with the Lord, and our reward with our God. Go on therefore in the midst of all your discouragements, and, in this respect, be not weary in well doing. Take heed of such a despair, as would cut the sinews of future endeavours. If your child were labouring under any bodily distemper, you would be very unwilling that the physicians should quite give him over, and try no farther medicines: You would follow them, and say, " can nothing more be done? Is there not the least glimmering of hope?" Alas! my friends, a child given up by a pious parent, is, to a believing eye, a much more melancholy fight, than a parent given over by the physicians. Excuse me, then, if I follow you with the question, "Can nothing more be done? Is there not the least glimmering of hope?" Who told you that the sentence of condemnation is sealed while you are sure it is not executed. Is the danger extreme? Let your efforts be so much the more zealous, your admonitions so much the more frequent and serious, your prayers so much the more earnest and importunate. And on the whole (to allude to the words of David on a much lower occasion) Who can tell whether God will be gracious, to you, that the child may live? and the sad apprehensions which you now entertain, may only serve to increase the joy with which you shall then say, this my son was dead, and is alive again; he was lost, and is found.

II. I would address myself to children: To you, the dear lambs of the flock, whom I look upon as no contemptible part of my charge. I have been speaking for you a great while, and now give me leave to speak to you; and pray, do you endeavor for a few minutes, to mind every word that I say.

You see that it is your parents' duty to bring you up for God. The great God of heaven and earth has been pleased to give his express command, that you should be trained up in the way in which you should go, even in the nurture and admonition of the Lord. It is the wonderful goodness of God to give such a charge: and methinks you should be affected with it, and should be enquiring what you should do in return.

Now there are three things which I would ask of every one of you, in return for this gracious notice which the great God has taken of you children: and I am sure, if you love your own souls, you will not deny me any of them:—Be willing to learn the things of God;—pray for them that teach you;—and see to it, you do not learn them in vain. Listen diligently, that you may understand, and remember each of these.

1. Be willing to learn the things of God.

The things of God are very delightful, and they are very useful; and, whatever you may think of it, your life depends on your acquaintance with them. So Christ himself says, this is life eternal, that they may know thee, the only true God, and Jesus Christ, whom thou hast sent. (John xvii. 3.) Therefore you children, should not think much of the labour of learning these things. Oh! far from that, you should be every day upon your knees, begging God that you may be taught to know him, and to know Christ. God has done a great deal more for you than he has for many others. You might have been born in a place where you never would have seen a bible in all your lives; where you would never have heard the name of Christ, where you might never have been instructed in the nature of duty and sin, nor have been told of the world beyond the grave; and so would probably have fallen into Hell before you had known there was such a place. And the great God has ordered matters so, that you are born under the light of the gospel, and have such plain and excellent instructions, that you may know more of divine things in your infancy, than the wise men amongst the heathens did, when they were old, and grey headed, and had spent all their lives in study. And will you be so ungrateful as not to be willing to learn, when such provision is made for your instruction? God forbid! Shall God give you his word, and your parents and ministers employ their time and their pains to teach you the meaning of it, and will you refuse to attend to it? That were foolish and wicked, indeed; I hope much better things of you. That is my first advice: Be willing to learn. I add,

2. Pray for those that are to teach you.

I would hope, that you little creatures dare not live without prayer. I hope God, who sees in secret, sees many of you on your knees every morning, and every evening, asking a blessing from him as your heavenly father. Now let me intreat you that at such times you would pray for those that instruct you in divine things: pray that God would bless them for it, and pray that he would help them in it. In praying thus for us, you do indeed pray for yourselves. There is a gracious promise to the people of God: *And they shall be all taught of God*: (John vi. 45.) Pray, that it may be fulfilled. Pray, that God would teach us to teach you; else we shall attempt it to very little purpose. Pray for your parents, and pray for your ministers.

Pray for your parents: That God would help them to instruct you in such a manner as they have now been directed: That they may do it plainly, so that you may be able to understand what they say; and seriously, that you may be brought to an holy awe of God; and tenderly that you may be engaged to love God and his word, and Christ and his ways; and pray that your parents may be stirred up to do it frequently, to give you *line upon line, and precept upon precept*, that you may be put in mind of what you are so ready to forget.

And let me desire you my dear charge, when you pray for your parents, to pray for your ministers too. I declare it again in the most public manner, it is my earnest desire that children would pray for me. And I verily believe every faithful minister of Christ would join with me in such a request. We do not, we dare not, despise the prayers of one of these little ones. Far from that, I am persuaded it would greatly revive, and encourage us, and we should hope God had some singular mercy in store for us, and his people, if we were sure the children of the congregation were every day praying for a blessing on our labours.

3. Take heed that you do not learn in vain. The great truths which you are taught from the word of God, are not intended merely to fill your heads with notions, but to

make your hearts and lives more holy. You know the way to your father's house, every step of it; but that would never carry you home, if you would not go in it. No more will it signify to know the way to heaven, unless we walk in it. *If you know these things,* says the Lord Jesus Christ himself, *happy are ye if ye do them.* And I may add, if ye do them not, it had been happier for you if you had never known them. Dear children, consider it; it is but a little while and you must die: And when those active bodies of yours are become cold, mouldering clay, the great God of heaven and earth will call your souls to his judgment seat. As sure as you are now in this house, you will shortly, very shortly, be standing before his awful throne. Then he will examine to what purpose you have heard so many religious instructions, so many good lessons. Then he will examine whether you have feared, loved, and served him, and received the Lord Jesus into your hearts, as your Saviour and your King: whether you have chosen sin or holiness for your way, earth or heaven for your portion. And if it be found that you have lived without thought, and without prayer, without any regard to the eye of God always upon you, and the word of God always before you, it will be a most lamentable case. You will have reason to wish, you had never heard of these things at all; for he has said, *the servant that knew his Lord's will, and did it not, shall be beaten with many stripes.* Even while I am speaking to you, death is coming on: perhaps his scythe may cut you down while you are but coming up as flowers. I speak to you thus plainly and earnestly because I do not know but you may be in eternity before another Lord's day. Oh! pray earnestly, that God would give you his grace to fit you for glory, and that all you may be so blessed that you may be made wise unto salvation by it. The Lord grant that it may!

And I have one thing to tell you for your encouragement, and then I have done with you for this time. How young soever you are, and how broken soever your heart may be, the glorious Lord of angels and men will be willing to hear what you say. You may be sure to be welcome to the throne of grace. The Lord Jesus Christ, when he was upon earth, was very angry with those who would have hindered little children from coming to him: He said, *Suffer little children to come unto me, and forbid them not, for of such is the kingdom of God.* And Christ is as compassionate now, as ever he was. Go to him, as you may humbly hope, he will, as it were, take you up in his arms and bless you. He has said it, and I hope you will never forget it; *I love them that love me, and they that seek me early shall find me.* Oh! were I but as sure, that every child in this assembly would go and ask a blessing from Christ, as I am that our dear Lord is willing to bestow it! But to draw to a conclusion.

III. I shall address myself to those young persons who are grown up to years of maturity, under the advantages of a religious education, and are not yet fixed in families of their own.

I hope that many of you have been sensible of the value of those opportunities you have enjoyed, and by divine grace have been enabled to improve them well; yet I must add, that I fear there are others amongst you who have unhappily neglected and abused them. I must apply myself distinctly to each of you.

To those young persons who have neglected and abused the advantages of a religious education.

I confess, there are hardly any to whom I speak with so little pleasure, because I have seldom less reason to hope I shall succeed. —What shall I say to you? What can I say that you have not often heard, and often despised? One is almost tempted, in such a circumstance, to turn reasonings and expostulations into upbraidings; and even to adopt those too passionate words of Moses, *"Hear now, ye rebels, you that have grown up in the knowledge, and yet the contempt of divine things; you that have disappointed the hopes, and slighted the admonitions of your pious parents, and so have broken their spirits, and, it may be, their hearts too, and have brought down their hoary hairs with sorrow to the grave.* One way or another you have perhaps *silenced them.* But it is a small thing to you that you have thus wearied men, and will you attempt to *weary your God also? Can you dare to hope, that you shall at last carry those proud, thoughtless heads triumphant over all the terrors of his word?"* You imagine it a very happy circumstance, that you have got loose from those mortifying lessons, and uneasy restraints, you were once under. But really, when one seriously considers whither these liberties lead you, and where they will probably end, a just resentment of your ingratitude is almost disarmed, and indignation is converted into pity.

Alas! Sinners, the way of all transgressions is hard; but yours is peculiarly so. You whom I am now addressing, are in the [morning] of your days, and it is not to be su[pposed] that the impressions of a good education [are] yet entirely effaced. What future years may do, I know not: but hitherto I persuade myself, you have frequently your reflections, and your convictions; convictions, which have force enough to torment you, though not enough to reform you; to plant thorns in the paths of sin, though not to reduce you to those of duty. But if you feel nothing of this remorse and anxiety, such a dead calm is then more dreadful than the fiercest storm of tumult and thought: A sad indication that your course in wickedness has been exceeding swift; indeed so swift, that it is probable it may not be long. Oh, that it might immediately be stopped by divine grace, rather than by the vengeance you have so much reason to fear!

At least be engaged to pause in it for a few moments, and let reason and conscience be permitted to speak. How is it that you make yourselves, I will not say entirely, but tolerably easy? Is it by the disbelief of christianity? Do you secretly suspect, that the gospel is but a cunningly devised fable? Yet even that suspicion is not enough. Let me rather ask, "Are you so confident it is so, that you will venture to stake even the life of your souls upon its falshood?" If you were come to such a confidence, yet it is amazing to me, how, even on the principles of natural religion alone, persons in your circumstances can make themselves easy. Can any of the libertines of the present age, that believe a God, imagine that he is altogether such a one as themselves? Can they flatter themselves so far as to hope, that they, in the ways of negligence, profaneness, and debauchery, are like to meet a more favorable treatment from him, than those pious parents whose principles they deride; or that this loose and irregular course will end better, than that life of prayer and self denial, of faith and love, of spirituality and heavenly-mindedness, which they discerned in them? Few are so abandoned, even of common sense, as to think this.

But these are more distant concerns. I bless God, this kind of infidelity is not in fashion here. You assent to the gospel as true, and therefore must know that God, who observes and records your conduct now, will bring you into judgment for it another day. And if you go on thus, how will you stand in that judgment? What will you plead? On what will you repose the confidence of your souls, that will not prove a broken reed, which will go up into your hand, and pierce you deep, in proportion to the stress you lay upon it? While you behave like a generation of vipers think not to say within yourselves, *We have Abraham for our father.* Think not to plead a relation to the religious parents, whose God, and whose ways you have forsaken. Think not to plead an early dedication to him in the baptismal covenant, which you have broken, despised, and in fact renounced. Think not to plead that external profession, which you have so shamefully contradicted, and even by wearing it, dishonored. You will see the weakness of such pleas as these, and will not dare to trifle with that awful tribunal, so far as to mention them there. And when you are yourselves thus silent and confounded, who will appear as an advocate in your favour? Your parents were often presenting their supplications and intercessions for you before the throne of grace, but there will be no room to present them before the throne of justice: Nor will they have any inclination to do it. All the springs of natural fondness will be dried up; they will no longer regard you as their children, when they see you in the accursed number of the enemies of their God.

And when you are thus difowned by your parents, and difowned by God, whither will you caufe your fhame and your terror to go? You, who have had fo many privileges, and fo many opportunities, perhaps I may add, fo many fond, prefumptuous hopes too, how will you bear to fee multitudes coming from carnal and profane families, to fhare with your parents in the inheritance of glory, from which you are excluded? You, who were the children of the kingdom; whofe remorfe therefore muft be the more cutting; whofe condemnation therefore muft be the more weighty! Obferve in how ftrong and lively a view our Lord has reprefented this awful thought in words which though immediately addreffed to the unbelieving Jews, are remarkably applicable to you: *There fhall be weeping and gnafhing of teeth, when ye fhall fee Abraham, Ifaac, and Jacob* (your pious anceftors) *in the kingdom of God, and yourfelves thruft out: And many fhall come from the North, and the South, and the Eaft, and the Weft, and fhall fit down with them in the kingdom of God; but the children of the kingdom fhall be caft out into utter darknefs.*

But through the divine forbearance you are not yet fhut out. There is ftill hope, even for you, if you will now return to the God of your fathers, from whom, by thefe aggravated tranfgreffions, you have fo deeply revolted. Let me then once more tenderly intreat you, and folemnly charge you by the confolation of the living, and by the memory of the pious dead, by your present comforts, by your future hopes, by the nearly approaching solemnities of death and judgment, by the mercies of God, and by the blood of a Redeemer, that you consider and shew yourselves men; that you set yourselves as it were, attentively to read over the characters inscribed on your memories and understandings in the course of a religious education; that you hearken to the voice of conscience, repeating those admonitions, and to the voice of the blessed God, as speaking in his word to confirm them; and finally, that you apply to him in a most importunate manner, for those victorious influences of his spirit, which are able to mollify, and transform these hearts of stone, and to raise even you, from so low a depth of degeneracy and danger, to the character and happiness of the genuine children of Abraham. God forbid that I should sin against your souls, and my own, in ceasing to pray that it may be so! And now,

2. I shall conclude all with an address to those young persons, who have been, through grace, engaged to a becoming improvement of the religious education they have enjoyed.

I have the pleasure of being well assured, that there are many such amongst you: Many who are now the joy of ministers and parents, and the hope of the church for succeeding years. Let me intreat you, my dear brethren and friends, that you daily acknowledge the divine goodness, in favouring you with such advantages; and what is still more valuable, in giving you a heart to prize and improve them.

Think how different your circumstances might have been. Providence might have cast your lot in some distant age or country, where the true God had been unknown, where your early steps had been guided to the groves and temples of detestable idols, and you might possibly have been taught to consecrate lust or murther by the name of devotion. Or you might have been educated in popish darkness, where the scripture would have been to you as a sealed book, and you would have seen christianity polluted with idolatrous rites, on some accounts more inexcuseable than those of the heathen, and adulterated with the most absurd and pernicious errors. There the mistaken piety of your parents might have proved a dangerous snare, whilst it had infused a blind, and perhaps a cruel zeal, and a proud, furious opposition to all the methods of better information.

Nay, even here in a protestant country, is it not too evident, there are many families in which had you been born and educated, you had sat as in darkness and the shadow of death, though in the land of light and the valley of vision? Your infant-tongue had been formed to the language of hell, and exercised in curses and oaths, rather than in prayer. You had early been taught to deride every appearance of serious godliness;

and all the irregular propensities of nature had been strengthened by examples of wickedness, which might have been sufficient to corrupt innocence itself. When you consider the wide difference between these circumstances and your own, surely whatever your portion of worldly possessions may be, you have reason to lift up your heads to Heaven with wonder and gratitude, and to say, *The lines have fallen to us in pleasant places, yea, we have a goodly heritage.*

Nor is this all: There are many around you, who have shared in such advantages as these, and have sinfully abused them, to the dishonor of God, to the grief of their parents, and to their own danger, and perhaps their ruin. And why are not you in that wretched number, or who maketh thee to differ from them? Why are not your hearts barred against the entrance of a Redeemer, but because the Lord has opened them? Why are not all the good instructions which have been given to you, like seed sown upon a rock; but because God gave the increase. Adore the riches of this distinguishing grace.

And let me earnestly exhort you, that you be careful still farther to improve it. Give me leave to say, that these fair openings of early seriousness, do naturally raise a very high expectation of eminent advances in religion. Let it be your humble and diligent care, that these expectations be answered: That your goodness may not be like the morning cloud, or the early dew, which soon goeth away; but rather like the dawning light, which shines brighter and brighter till the perfect day.

Whilst Providence continues these holy parents, to whom you have been so highly indebted, let it be your constant care, by all the most cheerful returns of duty and gratitude, to express your regards to them, and your sense of so great an obligation. And I will add, let it be your care, to hand down to future ages those important advantages you have received from them.

One generation passeth away, and another generation cometh. It is highly probable, that in a few years, numbers of you will be conducted into new relations; and we please ourselves with the hope, that you will carry religion and happiness into rising families. Let not those hopes be disappointed. When God fixes you in houses of your own, let it be your first concern to erect there such domestic altars, as those at which you have worshipped with such holy pleasure, and sensible tokens of divine acceptance. Let the sacred treasure of divine knowledge which has been deposited with you, be faithfully delivered down to your descendants; that they in their turn, may arise with the same pious zeal, to transmit it to another generation, that shall be born of them.

And may divine grace, that inexhaustible spring of the most valuable blessings, sweetly flow on to add efficacy to all, that real vital religion may be the glory and joy of every succeeding age; till this earth (which is but a place of education for the children of God, during their minority) shall pass away to make room for a far nobler scene and state of existence; where pious parents and their religious offspring shall forever enjoy the most delightful society inhabiting the palace of our heavenly father, and surrounding the throne of our glorified Redeemer!

A M E N.

www.ingramcontent.com/pod-product-compliance
Lightning Source LLC
Chambersburg PA
CBHW021946160426
43195CB00011B/1234